Managing

Grow

Roger Cartwri

■ **Fast track route to managing successful business growth**

■ **Covers the key areas of growth management, from understanding how organizations grow and the changes needed to facilitate growth, to mergers and acquisitions, franchising and alliances**

■ **Examples and lessons from some of the world's most successful high-growth businesses, including AOL, Dixons, Starbucks, and Wal-Mart, and ideas from the smartest thinkers, including Patricia Anslinger, Thomas Copeland, Peter Lorange, Noel Tichy, and Chris Zook**

■ **Includes a glossary of key concepts and a comprehensive resources guide**

≫EXPRESS EXEC.COM≪
essential management thinking at your fingertips

First published 2002 by
Capstone Publishing (a Wiley company)
8 Newtec Place
Magdalen Road
Oxford OX4 1RE
United Kingdom
http://www.capstoneideas.com

CIP catalogue records for this book are available from the British Library and the US Library of Congress

ISBN 1-84112-251-3

This book is printed on acid-free paper

Substantial discounts on bulk quantities of Capstone books are available to corporations, professional associations and other organizations. Please contact Capstone for more details on +44 (0)1865 798 623 or (fax) +44 (0)1865 240 941 or (e-mail) info@wiley-capstone.co.uk

Contents

Introduction to ExpressExec

ExpressExec is 3 million words of the latest management thinking compiled into 10 modules. Each module contains 10 individual titles forming a comprehensive resource of current business practice written by leading practitioners in their field. From brand management to balanced scorecard, ExpressExec enables you to grasp the key concepts behind each subject and implement the theory immediately. Each of the 100 titles is available in print and electronic formats.

Through the ExpressExec.com Website you will discover that you can access the complete resource in a number of ways:

» printed books or e-books;
» e-content – PDF or XML (for licensed syndication) adding value to an intranet or Internet site;
» a corporate e-learning/knowledge management solution providing a cost-effective platform for developing skills and sharing knowledge within an organization;
» bespoke delivery – tailored solutions to solve your need.

Why not visit www.expressexec.com and register for free key management briefings, a monthly newsletter and interactive skills checklists. Share your ideas about ExpressExec and your thoughts about business today.

Please contact elound@wiley-capstone.co.uk for more information.

Introduction to Managing Growth

» Growth is a natural function of both living things and organizations.
» Uncontrolled growth can be dangerous.
» Growth needs to be planned.
» Growth requires resources just as living things need nourishment.
» Growth should be incremental rather than spectacular.

Growth is something that, as living organisms, we are all used to. However it is not just living things that grow: organizations, whether in the public, the private, or the voluntary sectors, also grow. Just as human beings go through a life cycle, so do organizations.

Growth is something that has to be carefully regulated in the natural world. Too little growth and an organism cannot sustain itself or falls victim to predators. Too much growth in a population and the available food and territory resources become overstretched. Nature (with the exception of human populations) is very good at maintaining a balanced population.

Within our cells, uncontrolled growth has another more sinister name – cancer. Within organizations, uncontrolled growth can similarly lead to a series of problems that can eventually destroy the organization. Whilst owners and managers may want to see the organization grow and prosper they need to adopt strategies and tactics that allow them both to remain in control of the process and to ensure that the growth is reasonable: that does not become so rapid that it outstrips their ability to provide resources.

While it is often thought that companies go bust because of failure to compete, too much success can lead to the same tragic result. Unless a company controls its cashflow and its cost, uncontrolled growth can lead to a situation in which although there are plenty of orders, there is not enough cash to pay the bills (as will be demonstrated in Chapter 6). In such a situation, if creditors begin to demand payment and the cash is not there, the company may need to be sold despite its apparent success.

Growth needs to be planned and controlled. Effective managers and business owners are able to see the problems that growth can bring and deal with them. They know that it is sometimes better commercial sense to turn down business than to accept it. Accepting every opportunity for business that is offered may well provide short-term success but can lead to long-term financial problems and make the organization vulnerable to hostile attention from others seeking to grow by acquisition. Businesses often grow in the same way that humans do – by devouring other 'species' – and nobody wants to be eaten.

Using examples of companies such as America Online (AOL), Wal-Mart, Hyundai, Starbucks, and Dixons Group (UK), all of which have shown common sense in the way they have grown both within their home and other markets, this material is designed to allow you to analyze the environment for your own business, and plan growth that is both real and long term rather than a short-term success followed by disappointment.

There is a well-known prayer – applicable to any religion – which asks for:

> The courage to change the things one can change,
> The grace to accept those things that one cannot change
> And the wisdom to know the difference.

Managers and owners need the wisdom to look at growth very carefully and not to be dazzled by it, yet have the courage to do what is necessary and the grace to accept the rules of business – one of those rules being that there is a price for everything. As this material will describe, there are a number of ways to grow a business, some riskier than others. Successful business growth for the average operation is characterized by its incremental rather than spectacular nature, and this sometimes means applying the brakes rather than accelerating. For example, in the fictional work *Takeover*, by Peter Waine and Mike Walker, the progress of a business takeover battle is followed. An entrepreneur grows the company of which he is CEO by taking over a rival – but at a price. His board becomes so alarmed at his tactics for growth that they remove him. He gains the growth but loses the company he had founded.

This material is about how companies and other organizations grow. Advice is provided to ensure that growth is controlled and not so slow as to leave the company vulnerable to business predators or too swift and uncontrolled as to risk the operation becoming unmanageable. Very swift growth – *hypergrowth* – and its regulation are normally only effectively accomplished by large organizations with the internal resources to feed rapid expansion. This type of growth is the subject of a separate title in this series, *Strategies for Hypergrowth*.

What is Meant by Managing Growth?

» Growth occurs when an organization uses *transformation* to add value and uses the profits made to advance further additional activities.

» Growth can be achieved internally by increased activity or by acquiring other organizations.

» Organizations, like humans, products, and services, undergo a life cycle.

» Certain points in the life cycle are more conducive to growth activities than others.

» Organizations can enter periods of growth after apparent decline.

In everyday terms, *growth* implies that something – a person, an idea, or a company – is getting bigger. However it is actually more complicated than that.

THE TRANSFORMATION PROCESS

Organizations, whether in the private or the public sector, follow what can be called a transformation process, as shown in Fig. 2.1.

Fig. 2.1 The basic transformation process.

It is this transformation process that adds value. The nature of the inputs, transformation, and outputs will vary from sector to sector but in general terms they include the following.

Inputs

» Raw materials
» Components manufactured elsewhere
» Human skills and expertise
» Money
» Information
» Plant and equipment.

Transformations

» Manufacturing
» Data processing
» Service functions
» Analysis

Outputs

» Finished products
» Convenience

» Useable information
» Services
» Dividends to stockholders
» Profits
» Cash retained as investments
» Increased skills

THE FORMULA FOR GROWTH

Business operates to a simple formula:

> The cost of inputs + the cost of transformation should be less than(<) the value of outputs

That is, the transformation adds value to the inputs. Value is something that is actually determined by the customer. A supplier may say that their product or service is worth $50 but if customers will only pay $40 then that is what it is worth.

Let's take a simple example.

Company A stamps a piece of metal into a particular shape for passing on to Company B, which uses it as a component.

The *inputs* include the cost of the raw material, the wages of the employees, a proportion of the cost of the stamping equipment, the costs of energy, transport, finance, marketing, and support functions etc. The *transformation* – the act of stamping – adds sufficient value to the piece of metal that the customer (Company B) will pay enough for it – the *output* – to cover all the costs plus a margin to pay dividends and provide profit so that the company can invest in new equipment etc.

PROFIT PAYS FOR GROWTH

It is the profit element of the output that allows for growth. The management of growth is the management of profit. Profit can either be given to employees and the owners of the company (as dividends) or it can be invested in growth.

If this is managed carefully then a second transformation occurs, as shown in Fig. 2.2.

This material is concerned with the actions organizations need to take to ensure that profit is used wisely. It may be invested internally

Fig. 2.2 Transformation through investment.

in increased capacity, new procedures, or more staff. It can also be invested externally, either through pure investment in other companies where the organization takes a dividend, or by acquiring other operations.

ORGANIZATIONAL CHANGE

That products undergo a life cycle akin to the life cycle of living organisms is well known and understood. Organizations also undergo a similar life cycle. Cartwright (the writer of this material) and Green adapted the product life cycle as the concept of an organizational life cycle (Cartwright and Green, 1997). They suggested that organizations, like products go through a series of changes:

» birth
» adolescence
» maturity
» menopause
» decline.

They suggested that it was possible for changes at the menopausal stage to result in the aversion of decline, with the organization gaining a new, albeit different, lease of life – that is, renewed growth. This can be illustrated by Fig. 2.3.

In the context of managing growth, certain points in the organizational life cycle are very important.

Birth

At this stage a newly formed organization will be keen to gain customers and establish itself within the marketplace. Growth is not just desirable, it is a vital necessity.

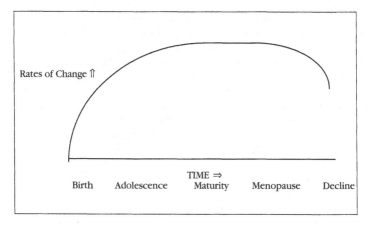

Fig. 2.3 Organizational life cycle, basic model (Cartwright and Green, 1997, with permission).

Birth is often a time when the organization and those who comprise it are at their most creative. The aim at the birth stage is to raise market awareness and to gain a degree of market share for the organization's products or services. There is a danger that the organization may promise more than it can deliver, either in terms of quality or demand exceeding supply. A new company may be relatively naive but be dealing with sophisticated customers. Customers may demand more and more in an attempt to gain greater value for less cost, and the organization may attempt to respond, with a resultant possible drain on its cashflows. An organization that wishes to survive into its adolescence needs to realize which changes it can encompass and which it cannot.

Adolescence

The adolescent organization is usually gaining both in confidence and sophistication and this represents one of the fastest periods of growth. Adolescent organizations are renowned for both their dynamism and the sense of enjoyment (and occasional frustration) enjoyed by those associated with them. The customer base is likely to be growing and the retention of existing customers becomes as important as the gaining of new ones, although this is something that is often forgotten, to the organization's cost. The organization will be developing a history and culture and can thus be more discriminating in the changes it is prepared to introduce. It is less likely to accept demands beyond its resources.

This can be a very dangerous time for an organization as it may be vulnerable to takeover by more established players seeking to grow, as Cartwright and Baird pointed out in 1999 in their study of the growth in the global cruise industry (Cartwright and Baird, 1999). Adolescent organizations often have cashflow problems associated with growth and a cash-rich competitor may attempt to gain control. An adolescent organization may be particularly vulnerable when faced with mature competitors. The acquisition of the highly successful but relatively young Princess Cruises (of *Love Boat*® television series fame) by the much older UK-based P&O Group in 1974 was a classic example of this; an acquisition that allowed P&O to achieve rapid growth in the important US market in a relatively easy manner.

Maturity

This is the time of greatest stability and thus a period when the organization may not want to make changes unless they are forced upon it. Growth is slow and may be only just enough to balance any decline. It is often at this time that an organization begins to take its customers for granted and becomes reluctant to accept the changes they require.

Menopause

Medically, doctors tend to say of the menopause that it may cause no problems at all or at its extreme may be characterized by hot flushes, tearfulness, anxiety, profound depression, inability to concentrate, inability to deal with problems, and inability to make decisions. Biologically, menopause is a condition built into the endocrinal (hormonal) system of the body and that it will occur is inevitable.

Menopause is often referred to in Western society as "The Change." It is not necessarily a change for the worse. It is reported that many women acquire new interests after menopause, and many organizations show a similar tendency to develop in new and exciting ways: in fact it can become a time of renewed growth.

There appears to be a menopausal stage in many organizations where, after a period of relative maturity, outside forces (the equivalent of the body's hormones) cause alterations in markets, technologies, and customer requirements. As with hormones in the body, the organization cannot control these forces and this may bring about inability in decision-making, a failure to deal with problems, organization anxiety, and depression. The organization becomes more interested in its own internal problems rather than those of its customers and any changes tend to be inwardly focused on systems and organizational structures in particular, rather than on the organization's products, services, and customers. Lethargy becomes a danger – a paradoxical danger because lethargy will destroy the organization yet takes hold just when the organization needs to concentrate on its position and survival. The main dangers are ultimate decline following a loss of customer base, or a takeover by a competitor. Indeed menopausal organizations may be most at risk from predatory adolescent organizations that have the energy but require the respectability of an older player in the market.

An organization that recognizes the menopausal stage can often take steps to rejuvenate itself and this may mean hard decisions. The aim is to become vibrant and entrepreneurial once more but the organization must ensure that the changes it makes are those its customers want. Often this is referred to as the organization *re-inventing itself*.

A model that more accurately reflects the complete organizational life cycle is shown in Fig. 2.4.

Decline

Organizations hope that they never decline but many do: to cite but a few examples, Pan Am, the US Passenger Shipping Industry, and many retail stores that were household names are no more. Some, like Pan Am, reappear as smaller-scale operations, while others are destined never to be heard of again – often they have been acquired by a more vibrant organization and the name has been lost.

If an organization cannot compete by making the changes that its customers require, it will decline and die or be swallowed up by a more successful competitor. Decline is often characterized by restructuring

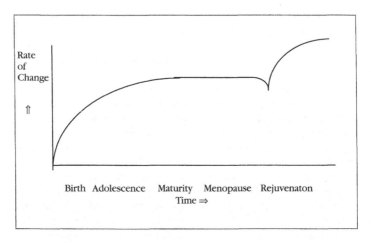

Fig. 2.4 Organizational life cycle, expanded model (Cartwright and Green, 1997, with permission).

upon restructuring, activity without growth, and frantic attempts to deliver something that will at least pay the wages, even if it does not make much – or any – profit for the company.

Rejuvenation

Rejuvenation is akin to rebirth and thus there is the opportunity to do new things and behave differently – to begin to grow again but in a different direction.

The importance of life cycle

The position of an organization is in its life cycle will affect its strengths and weaknesses and make some opportunities more important than others and some threats much more dangerous than others. It is easier to be entrepreneurial at birth and adolescence and also post menopause but only if decline is recognized and avoided.

KEY LEARNING POINTS

» Birth, adolescence and rejuvenation are the most conducive points of the organizational life cycle for growth activities.

» Decline can be made into rejuvenation and further growth, often in a new direction.

» Growth is funded by the value added by transformation.

» Adolescence, menopause and decline are periods of organizational vulnerability to cash-rich predators.

» Growth may be internal or by acquisition.

The Evolution of Growth Management

» The first forms of organizational growth occurred in the public sector, as rulers sought to provide for their subjects.
» Growth, as we know it today, needed different forms of finance to be developed.
» Investment in companies by the general population began to occur in the eighteenth century.
» Different industries have grown at different times in response to changes in the market.

It is the nature of human beings to be ambitious, and growth is an integral part of ambition.

THE BASIC AMBITION FOR GROWTH

Initially human tribes sought to grow by expanding their territory. More members of the tribe meant more land was needed for hunting and the growing of crops. Nature is very subtle about the methods used to regulate growth: populations and area are finely balanced. Too many individuals of any species eventually results in a lack of resources and, through hunger and famine etc., to a diminution in the population. Even where there is enough food, too rapid a growth in number can lead to stress and a reversal of growth, with numbers falling through attrition by stress-related diseases.

Using artificial means, humans have managed to grow and sustain far larger populations than nature would suggest possible, but as a species we seem unable to combat the effects of stress. In the developed world starvation and crippling epidemics may have been eliminated but strokes and heart disease have not. Nature still attempts to regulate growth.

Organizations, as shown in the previous chapter are subject to a life cycle and thus follow similar rules to living organisms, especially where growth is concerned. The problem of organizations becoming so large as to be unmanageable has been a comparatively recent one, but it is of considerable importance in modern times.

THE BASIC NATURE OF AN ORGANIZATION

The basic structure of an organization, with a leader and defined tasks carried out by those attached to the organization, is actually inherent in primate societies, of which humans are but one.

For any type of system to grow, the resources entering the system must be greater than those flowing out of the system. (In contrast, to reduce the size of a system, the formula must be reversed: less in = less growth. For example, medical authorities seem to be convinced that whatever miracle slimming aids come onto the market, the only effective method of losing weight is to reduce intake resources entering the system and/or increase activity to burn up one's intake.)

Organizations grow by taking in a number of different types of resources and – in the private sector at least – converting them into products or services and money. The money can then be used in four basic ways:

1 to buy more intake resources;
2 to pay for the process;
3 to pay the owners of the organization (i.e. the share/stock holders); or
4 to fund growth.

If the organization cannot provide the money for the first two options shown, it cannot survive in its current form as it will have to cut back on its activities. If it cannot pay any form of dividend (option 3) then its owners may wish to place their money elsewhere and if it cannot provide for growth (option 4) it will find it difficult to compete in the marketplace.

EARLY ORGANIZATIONAL GROWTH

Whilst the concept of trade is an old one in human societies, the concept of companies and corporations as we know them today is much more recent. Organizations can be defined as the structures human beings devise to carry out certain strategies. In the case of the private sector the ultimate goal is the making of money; in the public sector the provision of services to answer needs.

The earliest organizations were those of the public sector. As human societies became larger and moved away from close-knit family tribal groups, leaders had to set up structures to look after the needs of their subjects. Some of these groups became very large indeed, in fact they were empires.

The organization of the Roman Empire was a masterpiece. Throughout a geographic range stretching from Ireland to Africa the Romans instituted public works and a bureaucracy led by public officials. The key to their success was in part military but more to do with an efficient communication system. The Romans realized the importance of communication and built roads that were far better than anything that had been seen before, or were to be seen again for centuries after their decline.

Among the other empires of the ancient world were those of the Egyptians, Babylonians, and Persians, all of which preceded and were later supplanted by the Romans. The Phoenicians, who are generally acknowledged as the earliest overseas colonizers, established colonies along the shores of the Mediterranean Sea as early as 1100 BC, using the Mediterranean itself as their medium of communication. Phoenician colonization was motivated principally by the desire to expand and control trade. From the eighth century BC many of the Greek city-states expanded rapidly along the coasts of the north Aegean, the Black Sea, and southern Italy. The Greeks were driven by the need for arable land to sustain a growing population and the desire to facilitate commerce and trade. The city of Carthage, in present-day Tunisia, was founded as a Phoenician colony but eventually became an important colonial power itself, attempting to control Mediterranean trade by establishing a maritime empire that included colonies in Spain and Sicily. This brought Carthage and its empire into conflict with Rome, and in the third and second centuries BC, in the Punic Wars, the Romans defeated Carthage, laying the foundations of the huge empire that was to rule over much of Europe and the Middle East in the following centuries.

Following the collapse of Roman power in the fifth century AD, there was little growth beyond national/cultural boundaries during the Middle Ages, with the exception of the Scandinavian Vikings. They extended their domains considerably in the ninth and tenth centuries, establishing control over large areas of the British Isles and founding settlement colonies in Iceland, Greenland, and even Russia – perhaps as far south as Kiev. It has even been postulated that they reached North America via Greenland.

With the exception of the Church and the government, commercial-type organizations tended to be very small, family concerns. Even where a merchant or nobleperson owned large areas of land in different regions these tended to be treated as completely separate entities. Communication was not developed enough for control to be exercised from a distance. Those who owned land or industrial facilities appointed an agent and let that person get on with it – the owner's interest lay solely in collecting the money. Indeed for many noble families, trade was considered beneath their dignity. They would fund trading enterprises and take the profits but that was the limit of their involvement.

THE GROWTH OF MODERN ORGANIZATIONS

The growth of modern style organizations began with the voyages of discovery emanating in Europe from the fifteenth century onwards. Whilst some of the explorers may have been concerned purely with extending knowledge about the world, most of them were more concerned with commerce – they were seeking both new markets for their products and new products to sell to their home market, the proceeds of which would be used to repay those who had funded their expeditions.

These voyages were also responsible for the development of modern financing, without which organizations as they appear to today, especially in the private sector, could not function. The voyages were a partnership between the explorer and those who risked their capital on a successful venture rather than their lives. Whilst the original ventures tended to be single projects, with both cargo and ship being sold upon return to harbor, soon organizations began to develop as we know them today – organizations that existed longer than a single venture. While family firms had previously had this form of structure, larger projects had tended to be one-off affairs. Even wars were fought with armies that were disbanded as soon as peace was declared. Britain did not have a standing army until well into the nineteenth century. If war broke out there was a small core of regulars who had to be supplemented by troops recruited for the occasion. Such one-off project operations still occur today: the forming of TML (Trans Manche Link) to build the Channel Tunnel between the UK and France in the 1980s and early 1990s is an example.

In the Middle Ages, most businesses were local in nature, as the logistics for overland travel were difficult. European explorers soon came to find that they were not unique in the way they organized their economies and society: they discovered thriving civilizations in China, India, and South America. Initially only in the case of South America did the Europeans, driven by thoughts of gold and conversion to Christianity, seek to overthrow the rulers and take over. With China and India the Europeans were initially content to set up trading stations in the coastal areas.

As sea travel was the easiest means of moving goods it was ports that became the fastest growing towns and cities, including London and Bristol in England, Boston and New York in the American Colonies (as they were then), and the Hanseatic ports on the Baltic. Until well into the seventeenth century the only national organizations were the ruler and the Church – the logistic of setting up national commercial organizations either in terms of transport or financing did not exist.

THE EFFECT OF COLONIZATION

Colonization led to a massive growth in trade of all forms. Goods needed to be transported to the ports, ships had to be built and supplied – the spin-off effects benefiting a large number of people. Initially, trade voyages were financed by rulers and governments to supplement their coffers and to pay for military expeditions, etc. The voyages of Sir Francis Drake were at the behest and for the profit of the English Queen, Elizabeth I. Before long, however, wealthy merchants began to finance such trade, often forming syndicates to finance particular voyages and to share out the profits. Whilst the sailors took physical risks, the financial risks to the merchants were in fact small when compared to the fantastic profits that could be made. As in all commercial activity, the merchants were supplying a growing customer demand for luxuries and unusual items. On both sea and land large quantities of goods and people (as the slave trade grew as an unfortunate and tragic consequence) were moving around the globe.

An investor with money could share vicariously in the excitement of the age by putting money into a trading venture and with luck would make a profit. These ventures were not like the incorporated or joint stock companies of today: at the end of each venture the syndicate would divide all of the profits and dissolve. This was a very inefficient method of managing increasing large commercial ventures and thus organizations (companies) were set up to exist beyond a particular venture. Many of these companies sought investment not just from wealthy private benefactors but also from a growing middle class made prosperous by the very growth in trade it was now helping to finance. Unfortunately the early stock market was even more volatile than it is today, and after the South Sea Bubble fiasco of 1720 the British government began to regulate trade and its financial aspects more rigorously.

The South Sea Bubble plan was devised by the Robert Harley, Earl of Oxford, in 1711, as a method to pay off Great Britain's national debt. Under the plan, the debt was assumed by merchants to whom the government guaranteed for a certain period annual payments equal to $3mn. This sum, amounting to 6% interest, was to be obtained from duties on imports from certain areas, namely the Pacific Ocean trade that was just beginning to be developed. The monopoly held by sections of British trade in the South Seas and South America was given to these merchants, incorporated as the South Sea Company, and extravagant ideas of the riches of South America and the South Seas were fostered to attract investors. This early example of commercial hype was probably the first time attempts were made to raise capital by presenting a rosier picture than was actually the case (but certainly not the last). In the spring of 1720 the company offered to assume practically the whole national debt, at that time equal to more than $150mn. Companies of all kinds were floated to take advantage of the public interest in obtaining South Sea Company stock. Speculation soon carried stock to 10 times its nominal value despite there being no actual earnings at the time. The chairman and some directors sold out, the bubble burst, and the stock collapsed.

Thousands of stockholders were ruined. Parliamentary investigation revealed complicity by some company officials and other public notables including members of the royal court of George I. However, a political crisis was averted through the efforts of Sir Robert Walpole, who at that time was serving as Chancellor of the Exchequer and later became the first person to hold a post equated with that of the present-day British Prime Minister. Only about 33% of the original capital was recovered for the stockholders.

Despite this failure the public soon took to this form of investment and organizations were able to raise money through ownership rather than borrowing. This greatly aided those with new ideas and who could convince investors to take a modest risk with them. Investors were spreading individual risk by their weight of numbers and thus facilitating the growth of companies.

THE INDUSTRIAL REVOLUTION

The industrial revolution that began in Britain at the beginning of the nineteenth century was a time when companies had the opportunity to grow at a far greater rate than in the past. The building of a rail network, first in Britain and the eastern seaboard of the US, and then throughout Europe, ensured that goods and people could be transported swiftly and safely in a fraction of the time previously possible. From a twenty-first-century viewpoint with aircraft traveling at anything up to twice the speed of sound it is perhaps difficult to comprehend the difference that rail travel brought, especially in Europe where distance between major population and manufacturing centers are less than in the US. By 1890 the British rail network was complete and there were few if any towns or even villages (and perhaps of greater importance, factories and warehouses) more than five miles from the nearest station except in more remote areas. In 1865 at the end of the American Civil War there were 35,000 miles of track in use in the US, by 1888 this number had increased by a factor of over four, to 156,000. The national expansion of large organizations was now possible. The railroads, together with the shipping companies that were moving increasing numbers of emigrants across the Atlantic, were amongst the largest of these new industrial giants, as were the iron and steel works, mining, engineering, and chemical plants that were being developed at an increasing rate. The scale of the engineering projects was such that small companies could not meet the needs and thus had to grow either organically within themselves or by merger and acquisition.

THE TWENTIETH CENTURY

By 1914 there were many very large companies supplied by a myriad of smaller ones. Growing populations had led to the growth of both manufacturing and service industries. The increasing militarism in Europe had also resulted in growth among those companies that supplied the means of waging war. Shipyards had never been busier. World War I put the expansion plans of many companies on hold, with those of companies located in the Triple Alliance (Germany, Austro-Hungary, and Turkey) such as Krupp, I.C. Farben, and Skoda to be shelved for decades. By 1918 the days of coal as the prime source of energy were over: the world had become an oil-based economy and this had an effect on the growth of companies in the country that was soon to be the world's major economic power – the US.

The US government that had been so suspicious of trusts and cartels before the war now changed its stance as the need to secure oil supplies became apparent. The US government began to secure the nation's supplies by actively *encouraging* such syndicates of oil companies. Collier and Horowitz (1976) have commented that the US government was actually orchestrating the formation of a powerful syndicate of US oil companies abroad. Whereas in the past such syndicates would have been illegal, the government refused to assist Standard Oil in expanding into Mesopotamia on its own, insisting that a syndicate be formed.

The world was hit by the great depression between the wars and many smaller companies were taken over. The foundations for the future large corporations were being laid.

RECENT GROWTH

The twentieth century saw a huge growth in the engineering sectors. In more recent times the growth industries have been those connected with ICT (Information and Communication Technology), services, and the vacation sector. As disposable incomes and leisure times increase, so those industries that cater for leisure activities have tended to grow.

Different eras have presented different growth patters. They all have three things in common however:

» they require adequate resources;
» their process adds value; and
» they meet the needs of their customers.

These are the main prerequisites for growth. The resources may change, as will the needs, but no company can grow if it cannot acquire the necessary resources or if it does not meet its customers' needs. The growth in the railway companies and amongst e-mail providers is actually very similar. Using the best technology available at the time they have both met a need for enhanced communications. The railways eventually declined in the face of road and air competition – will the same happen to e-mail and Internet providers?

Fig. 3.1 shows a timeline of the development of organizations and their management of growth.

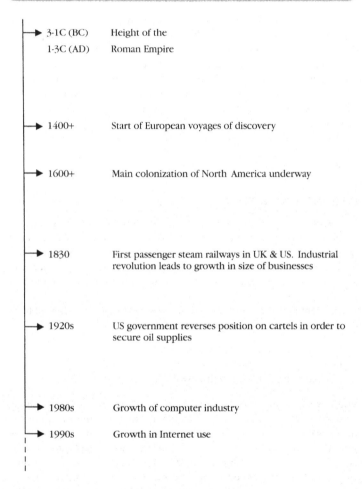

Fig. 3.1 Timeline of of growth of organizations.

LEARNING POINTS

» In order to grow companies need both finance and markets.
» Effective communication is an important factor in managing organizational growth.
» Different industries and sectors grow at different times.

The E-Dimension of Managing Growth

» Many businesses have used the Internet to facilitate their growth.
» A Web presence is now an expected norm.
» As faith in the security of payment systems over the Internet grows, so will e-commerce.
» The Internet has provided a growth opportunity for organizations providing Internet-linked services and products.
» It is no use gaining new customers via the Internet (or any other means) if increased demand cannot be met.
» A Webpage may be the first contact a potential customer has with an organization and so must be of high quality.

The Internet has been a vehicle for growth in many areas of business. Whilst some companies owe their very existence and growth to the Internet and connected computer developments – AOL (America On Line), the subject of the best practice section at the end of this chapter, is one of these – others have used e-commerce to support more traditional methods of business.

No modern organization wishing to grow can afford not to have a Web presence, as this is where many potential customers now go in order to find out about the organization and its products. There are online catalogues available on the Internet for everything from furniture and computers to model railroad equipment. These online catalogues have the advantage that they can be much more up to date than a printed version. More and more companies are including details of their commitments to the environment and the community on their Websites so that customers and potential customers can get a feel for the philosophy of the company.

The Internet has rapidly become a major means of communication between organizations and their customers, as well as providing internal communication within the organization and an important link to its suppliers. Effective communication is a prerequisite of growth. As faith in the security of payment systems grows, more and more customers are using the Internet to make purchases, thus removing barriers of geography for an increasing number of organizations.

There has been a dramatic growth in organizations providing and maintaining Websites and in the supply of Internet service generally. A new method of doing business sparks growth in new companies that believe that they can find a niche and older ones seeking to use their expertise in a new manner. Christopher Price has profiled a number of new entrepreneurs in his book *The Internet Entrepreneurs*. It is quite staggering how many new companies the Internet has given birth to and the speed with which many are growing.

The suppliers of hardware also benefit from this growth. There are few offices in the world without a personal computer in them and in the developed world the same is true of homes. The British Prime Minister, Tony Blair, has stated that he wants every school in the country to be "online" in the early years of the twenty-first century, so important is the so-called knowledge economy that is being driven by the Internet.

In addition to the suppliers of hardware there are also growth opportunities for software developers. Microsoft and Lotus (now part of IBM) are global names almost as well known as Coca-Cola. Suppliers of anti-virus software, such as Symantec (who offer Norton and other products) have gained global prominence as they devise and release products to combat what has become the global menace of destructive computer viruses. The suppliers of the essential but more mundane items such as discs, cables, and printer paper have also been able to grow their business as computer and Internet use increases.

GROWING VIA THE E-DIMENSION

Any organization that wishes to grow its customer base will find that the Internet is a useful tool. There are, however, a number of steps that the organization must take to ensure that the investment in technology will be rewarded.

1 Ensure that any increased demand for products or services generated by a growth in the customer base can actually be met. Stimulating demand and then not being able to satisfy it often leads to potential customers going to a competitor. Having had their demand stimulated the customer is going to try and acquire the product and if the original organization cannot meet the need there will soon be a competitor who can: the original organization has thereby lost a potential customer, perhaps for ever.

2 Make sure that the Website is carefully designed to show off the organization's products and services to the best advantage. A poorly designed Website is probably worse than none at all. The Webpage may be the potential customer's first encounter with the organization and first impressions are very important.

3 Be able to satisfy customers of the security of payment systems, especially that their debit, credit, or charge card details will be safe.

4 Set up a logistics operation to deliver products to the customer.

5 Set up a customer care operation that can respond to customers wherever they may be located. One of the most frequently stated customer concerns about buying online is "What happens if it goes wrong?"

6 Study the consumer and safety legislation in those areas it is desired to serve. Tailor procedures to meet them.

7 Make sure that any equipment is compatible with the area being served. For example, European countries use 220–240V electric supply and do not have standardized plug fittings. North American video cassettes will not work on many European TV and video sets (although dual use machines are now on the market).

8 Design the operation and procedures in such a manner as to make updating with new technology as easy as possible.

These simple considerations will assist in making the operation more customer friendly and therefore more attractive. If growth becomes large then it may well be worth setting up a local agency and perhaps a more indigenous operation, as, for example, Amazon.com has done with Amazon.co.uk and its other operations outside the US.

INTERNET-SPECIFIC COMPANIES

There are some companies that have grown as a direct result of the development of the Internet and computer technology. The companies developing search engines have shown rapid growth (a number of them are profiled by Price in *The Internet Entrepreneurs*): Yahoo!, Lycos, AltaVista, Excite, etc. are now global names and provide an essential link between that other growth area, the Internet Service Provider (ISP) – such as AOL, featured later in this chapter – the Internet customer, and the Webpage. To be used properly, the Internet needs all these components to be working in unison. While consumers generally pay for ISP services (although they are free in some countries), search engines usually are funded through advertising.

The growth of companies such as Microsoft, Dell, and other computer giants stems from the connectivity between operating systems, software, telecommunications, and the Internet. Amazon.com has, in effect, made every purchaser of books and other products from its site a branch of the organization. By feeding back preferences into the system, Amazon are able to offer increased added value on the next visit by suggesting items that the customer might enjoy. It is this synergy that makes the Internet such a potent vehicle for growth.

Companies that offer Internet-related services have seen rapid growth and some have also seen decline. As with any new technology the organizational life cycle, as covered in Chapter 3, tends to see winners and losers. The companies that have succeeded have been those whose growth has been carefully linked to customer demand. The attempt to introduce WAP mobile telephones in the UK during 2000 and early 2001 was not as successful as had been hoped, mainly due to the fact that customers did not perceive the need for the technology as yet. It may well be that they will be more convinced some time in the future.

Companies wishing to offer Internet-related services need to remember that, although the technology may be new, growth occurs because traditional business rules are followed, at least in part. Finance has to be secure. Quality must be high and customer care put at the center of the operation. Customers are becoming ever more sophisticated and whilst the first generation of Internet users may have tolerated bugs and crashes, the current and future generation expect things to work on as near to zero defect as possible.

BEST PRACTICE: AOL (AMERICA ON LINE)

One might expect an Internet Service Provider with the name AOL to do well and grow in the US, but what about the rest of the world?

Why should people in, say, the UK decide to sign up with an ISP that obviously foreign? The only reason anybody does something like that is because they receive value for money and excellent service.

When AOL was formed in 1985 the number of users of personal computers was very small but growing. In the UK, the government was in the process of implementing its first program of putting computers within schools. The three choices were a Research Machines (RML) 480Z, a metal cased, robust machine; the popular BBC Model B; or a Sinclair Spectrum. None of the three had a hard disk; all programs were loaded via cassette recorder. Primitive as they were, they provided hands-on computer experience for a generation that was to grow up with the computer as a part of daily life.

By 2001 it was difficult to find a home in any developed country whose members did not have access to a personal computer (PC) either at home or at work – or increasingly both – and who had not experienced the Internet. AOL alone has 29 million users of its branded AOL services.

For those at the cutting edge of the computer revolution it was becoming clear as early as the mid-1980s that the real growth area in usage would be the synergy of linked computers to pass information. In was in 1985 that Steve Case and Jim Kinnsey set up a company, Quantum Computer Services, to deliver online information via computer modems. Steve Case set a contest for a new name for the company in 1989 and promptly won it himself with the name America On Line (AOL). AOL offered information, games, and a new service for the public: e-mail, with the possibility to communicate with other members electronically. E-mail had been around in a commercial setting throughout the latter part of the 1980s but mainly only within corporate networks with few means of communicating outwith the corporate boundaries. Now it was becoming available in the public domain.

AOL's marketing was highly successful. The company began the concept of giving away its software, attaching it to the covers of computer magazines and even through mailshots. The company was the first, in 1993, to offer a version of their software that ran on Microsoft's Windows® platform, which was fast becoming the global norm. By 1994 there were one million AOL members and the company linked them to the Internet for the first time using AOL.com. The IPO for AOL was in 1992 and in 1995–96 the company expanded abroad, launching services in the UK, Germany and Canada with local news etc. covered on its various sites.

CompuServe, a competitor ISP, was acquired in 1998, the year in which AOL carried more messages than the US Postal Service. The power and strength of e-mail as a global communication medium was by now growing rapidly, having moved from the purely commercial into the domestic market as well. The innovative ICQ operation, allowing users to let others know when they are online, plus the provision of chat facilities, was also acquired that year. By 1999, ICQ had tripled its number of members since acquisition to 40 million in only 14 months. Netscape (the Internet browser developed by Netscape Corp.) was just one of a number of brands to come under the AOL banner in 1999, the year in which AOL Hong Kong was launched.

By 2000, having expanded into Latin America (AOL Mexico and AOL Argentina) there were 27 million global AOL users with a new one joining the service on average every six seconds.

Momentous developments were in the wings. On January 11, 2001 AOL merged with Time Warner, the entertainment and media group (incorporating both the Time and Warner Brothers corporations.) Time's ancestry goes back to 1922, whilst that of Warner Brothers stretches back to 1918, the end of World War I. The synergy between publishing, music, movies, and the Internet is a powerful one.

By the time of the merger the number of AOL members was approaching 30 million and the company was operating in 16 countries and in 8 different languages.

Having developed a strategic alliance with Sun Microsystems, AOL was a major force in the global communication arena.

Constantly being updated, AOL's products have met the needs of users across the globe despite the nationalistic nature of the name. Growth has been steady and always such as to build on synergy. Simultaneously, AOL has grown by developing new products (organic growth), acquisitions, and geographic growth, to provide a one-stop solution for the Internet needs of its growing number of members.

As David Stauffer points out in *Business the AOL Way* (2000), in the eight years between the IPO and 2000, AOL stock appreciated by almost 69,000%. The market valuation of AOL in 2000 was greater than that of all the publicly traded US newspaper industry, evidence of how important the Internet and its associated products have become.

Stauffer provides ample evidence in the form of quotes to suggest that there were those who did not believe that AOL would be a success – at one time it was doubted whether it could outperform CompuServe. However, AOL is a company that has been prepared to meet challenges. By providing for a user's entire Internet needs (if he or she so wishes) within an easy-to-use framework, AOL inspires customer loyalty. The regularity by which the necessary upgrades are sent to the user and the imaginative pricing schemes to suit national conditions also engender loyalty. For example, in the UK one can choose a series of pricing plans depending on the usage made of the service, and there is a freephone access number.

In 2001 in the US, AOL experimented with providing a PC with which to access the Internet. CompuServe users in the US have been offered a free PC following a deal with eMachines. While users in other countries did not receive the same offer it was noteworthy that the UK PC warranty company Direct Care almost immediately offered a PC to members of their Online Direct ISP service for £299 instead of the normal £450. It may well be that the growth business is now in the ISP market rather than the PC market. This does make good business growth sense. Users who receive a free or heavily discounted PC will, so the wisdom goes, then spend much more with the ISP providing the hardware. The costs to the ISP are not that high, the cost price of entry-level PCs having dropped rapidly over recent years.

Perhaps one of the reasons for AOL's success is the fact that it does not view itself as a technology company. It is a service company that allows people to access the fastest growing communication and information medium – the Internet. By concentrating on service rather than technology, AOL is able to relate most closely to its members, the vast majority of whom are technology users but not necessarily technically minded. It is very easy and inexpensive to access one's AOL e-mail service from any Internet-connected terminal in the world, which means that members never need to be out of touch. This is a similar philosophy to that which has accounted for the success of Apple and Microsoft – they realize that things have to be made easy for the customer. They do the hard work; the customer reaps the benefit.

KEY LEARNING POINTS

» The Internet can facilitate growth both for companies that use it as a tool and also for those formed to supply products and services for it.

» There is no point in stimulating a demand that cannot be met - that just drives potential customers to competitors.

» A Website is as important as other factors in promoting an organization's image. A poorly designed Website will leave a bad impression of the organization in the mind of a potential customer.

The Global Dimension of Growth Management

» Business, amongst other things, is done differently in other countries, and this must be kept in mind when planning to grow by global expansion.
» Local culture must be taken into account when growing on a global basis.
» The Starbucks model of incremental linked steps in global expansion coupled with steady growth in the original market carries fewer risks than an attempt to penetrate global markets too swiftly.

Not all companies will wish to extend their operations outside their own national borders but, as covered in the previous chapter, the Internet has made the acquisition of a global customer base much easier. Those organizations that can supply their products or services online (by download) have no obvious distribution problems, but more and more retailers are discovering that, thanks to global delivery services such as UPS or FedEx, a global operation is a possible growth area for even the smallest company.

ISSUES OF GLOBAL EXPANSION

When companies decide to grow by undertaking operations outside their national area, the major issues facing them are *procedural* and *cultural*.

Differences in procedure

Procedures for finance, credit, customs regulations, sales taxes, etc. vary from one jurisdiction to another even within economic areas such as the EU (European Union) and NAFTA (North American Free Trade Agreement). Any business considering growth outside its own national borders should consult the trade department of its own government and the trade representatives at the nearest embassy or consulate of the country where the business is to be conducted. This will assist in contacting local lawyers and agents. The company's bankers are also likely to have important and useful contacts.

Cultural concerns

The second issue is that of working in a different *culture*. Culture can be defined as the "way we do things around here" and differs from place to place across the globe, between ethnic groups, and between organizations. There is, fortunately, a wealth of material on managing cultural differences and the reader is advised to consult Chapters 5 and 6 of *Managing Diversity* (in this *ExpressExec* series), *Riding the Waves of Culture* by Fons Trompenaars, *When Cultures Collide* by Richard D Lewis, and *Managing Cultural Differences* by Philip Harris and Robert Morgan (details of each of these are given in Chapter 9). The latter two texts provide information on business habits across the world together with information on how - and how *not* - to behave).

There are a whole range of cultural issues that a company needs to consider if expansion into another area of the world is being proposed. These include:

» what form of hierarchy does the culture encourage or accept;
» what are its attitudes to gender;
» what are its attitudes to age and experience;
» who makes buying decisions;
» what is acceptable and not acceptable in advertising copy;
» what employment rights and legislation exist;
» whether its business practices oppose or differ from those in the organization's home country;
» what procedures exist for making complaints;
» what consumer protection legislation exists; and
» what arrangements exist for financial protection.

It may well be that some of the above run counter to the company's own beliefs and culture. Most organizations based in developed countries have a policy relating to equal opportunities, this is not always the case elsewhere. The company, by being sensitive, can perhaps use their policies to encourage change and enlightenment – something that Anita Roddick encouraged in The Body Shop. Bribery is against the law in most developed countries, whereas in some parts of the world "commissions" are the expected and accepted way of doing business. More than one business person has fallen foul of this when working abroad, through doing business in a way acceptable to (and possibly expected by) local organizations – although not acceptable or even legal in his own country – and then being criticized and punished for it on his or her return home.

Advertising can be another area where culture clashes can occur. There have been examples of advertisements that have been truly global in nature but they have been few and far between. Nike, the British Airways "Global" advertisement featuring people from all over the world making a globe, and the famous "I'd like to buy the world a Coke" advertisements for Coca-Cola worked almost everywhere. Others often need to be customized for the particular culture. Even within the English-speaking world there are considerable cultural and subtle linguistic differences.

It is not difficult to discover the cultural norms of an area and it is nearly always worth taking the time to do so. Suppliers, customers, and employees will always be happier with a company, product, or service that they feel comfortable with, and the more the organization and what it offers is in tune with cultural norms, the more comfortable people will be and thus the more likely they are to give their business to the company.

Moving into a foreign market can be an exciting way of growing but it is best to remember that things may not be as they are at home. Perhaps the wisest course of action is to move in small incremental steps and make the operation as near to indigenous as possible. Use local phrases, suppliers, and staff and the people locally will begin to think of the company as a local one and not a foreign intruder.

With the exception of Coca-Cola, its rival Pepsi, hamburgers (especially McDonald's), and Kentucky Fried Chicken, food items are sometimes the hardest to place in an alien culture. Food is a very important part of culture, partly because many religions have very strict rules about what can and cannot be eaten, and thus the purchasing decision of the customer involves more than just taste. Apart from the successful US companies mentioned above, there is one other that deserves mention as having taken a fairly mundane foodstuff into a global market with considerable success – the company is Starbucks and the commodity is coffee.

BEST PRACTICE – STARBUCKS

In many ways Washington State is far from the seat of power in the US. However, the State and its major conurbation, Seattle, are home to some of the best-known global names in commerce, three of which – Amazon.com, Microsoft, and Boeing – have become household names. Despite the perception of the "Northwest Corner effect" giving the area its insular nature, there must be something in the water that promotes growth ... or perhaps it is in the caffeine, for Seattle is also the home base of Starbucks, a US and increasingly worldwide icon for coffee drinking.

Once just a single outlet on the Seattle waterfront, by the end of the twentieth century there were over 1600 Starbucks stores scattered across the world, with a new one opening its doors each day.

Starbucks' first store was opened by Jerry Baldwin, Gordon Bowker, and Zev Siegl in 1971. It was not the best time to start up a business in Seattle as Boeing, the major employer in the area, was in financial difficulties and laying off staff – prompting the famous billboard "will the last person to leave Seattle please turn off the lights." Interestingly, the story of that billboard appears not only in books about Boeing (Irving quotes it in *Wide Body*, his study of the building of the Boeing 747) but also in *Pour Your Heart into It*, by Howard Schultz, the chairman and chief global strategist of Starbucks. The three founders of Starbucks were coffee lovers – proper coffee, that is, not the bland products that were filling supermarket shelves at the time. That the three men had struck a chord at the right time is evidenced not only by the success of Starbucks but also by the success of other similar operations. Previously unknown, Costa Coffee shops began to appear on high streets, railway stations, and airport terminals in the UK in the 1990s, showing how consumers were seeking authentic tastes. Initially Starbucks was simply a supplier of high quality coffee products, rather than the now familiar coffee shop operation it has become.

Zev Siegl sold out his holding in 1980 and in 1982 Howard Schultz joined the company as the director of retail operations and marketing (now chairman and chief global strategist). Visiting Italy, Schultz decided that the "expresso bar" culture might go down well in Seattle and started Il Giornale, a coffee bar operation using beans from Starbucks. This proved so successful that, in 1987, Il Giornale acquired Starbucks' assets; the name of the company was changed to the Starbucks Corporation, and outlets opened in Chicago and Vancouver, Canada – just across the border from Washington State. By then Starbucks had grown to 17 outlets.

Growth in another direction occurred in 1988 when the company began a mail order operation encompassing the whole of the US, while further increasing their number of outlets – now 33. Mail order brought the Starbucks name to a much wider audience.

In considering staff needs, in 1991 Starbucks became the first privately owned US company to offer stock options to part-time employees. The nature of the coffee shop business is such as to attract a considerable number of part-time employees and this type of recognition is an important motivator, showing that such staff are considered as much a part of the organization as those working full time. The care for staff is undoubtedly one reason why the number of outlets grew almost fourfold between 1988 and 1991 (from 33 to 116). Starbucks' IPO was completed in 1992, the year in which the company gained the important Nordstrom account and continued its expansion by opening more outlets in California and Colorado, bringing the total to 165, a number that further doubled the next year, including the first outlet in Washington, DC.

Also in 1993 Starbucks began its relationship with the book-selling giant, Barnes and Noble. Whilst books and coffee might seem a strange synergy, it is not really so unusual – many book-stores were already offering coffee to browsers. Coffee and reading go together exceptionally well, and Starbucks has also formed relationships with the Canadian bookseller Chapters, and has become involved with a number of literary projects.

Whilst the move into an adjacent part of Canada was predictable, Starbucks' next area of international growth was to a market that might not be immediately associated with a US or European-style coffee shop operation. A 1995 joint venture with Sazaby Inc was completed to develop a chain of Starbucks stores in Japan. With additional US outlets opening in a number of major cities in 1995, the total number of Starbucks stores reached 676. The Japanese coffee shops opened in 1996, together with outlets in Hawaii and Singapore. Starbucks also introduced ice cream sales and negotiated a partnership with PepsiCola to sell a bottled version of Starbucks' Frappuccino® blended beverage. The number of outlets reached 1015. The next year the company expanded into the Philippines, with further growth into Thailand, New Zealand and Malaysia in 1998.

If one examines the way Starbucks had grown to this point, it can be seen that most (but not all) of the growth was to the west and south of Washington State, moving across the Pacific into regions where either there was a considerable US influence or English was a common language – Japan, the Philippines, New Zealand, etc.

The Seattle Coffee Company had been developing a similar concept, with 60 outlets in the UK. It does not follow that UK tastes will exactly mirror those of the US but there are cultural and, of course, linguistic similarities. By acquiring the UK operation in 1998, Starbucks made an important move into the wider European market. 1999 and 2000 saw the Starbucks concept extended, both geographically – into China, Dubai (in the Persian Gulf), Hong Kong (by then under Chinese control but still retaining considerable Western influence), Kuwait, South Korea, and Lebanon – and in terms of concept: it had introduced new types of outlets and also moved into groceries, through an agreement with Kraft, and music sales.

Another important move in 2000 was Starbucks' alliance with Trans Fair USA to market and sell "Fair Trade" certified coffee in over 2000 outlets. Concern about fairness to coffee growers has been but one part of wider concerns about globalization and the domination of food supplies by large corporations. By signing this agreement, Starbucks sent a very powerful message to others in the business world. Plans for 2001 included further European growth into Switzerland and Austria in partnership with Swiss Bon appétit Group AG. It is expected that there will be 15 Swiss stores by 2003, plus a number in Austria.

Starbucks' growth has been logical and its global moves were carefully chosen to ensure success. They can be summarized as shown in Table 5.1.

One of the difficulties of growing a company such as Starbucks is the reliance on a single product – coffee. A bad harvest can have a devastating effect even if it is not in an area from which the company sources its products. Such a problem occurred in 1994, when the Brazilian coffee crop was blighted by severe frost. Starbucks did not use Brazilian coffee but, as Brazil traditionally supplies over 25% of the world's coffee, a shortage in Brazil would

Table 5.1 The growth of Starbucks.

Year	Expansion into	Total outlets
1971	Seattle	1
1987	US, Canada	17
1988–95	US	676 (1995)
1996	US, Japan, Hawaii, Singapore	1015
1997	US, Philippines	1412
1998	US, UK	1886
1999	US, Canada, China, Kuwait, South Korea, Lebanon	2135
2000	US, Dubai, China	3300

drive up the price on the world market. With over 300 outlets, Starbucks would be hit heavily by such a price hike. The last similar situation had been 20 years earlier, at a time when Starbucks had only three stores - 1994 was going to be difficult. The problem for Starbucks was a medium-term one. The company already had advance purchases that would last for nearly a year but should it continue to buy as the price rose? If it did not, it was possible that others would and that there would be problems supplying the operation after the year had passed. There was also the issue of what to do about the price charged in the outlets - when should it rise and by how much?

The decision was made not to raise prices immediately. However a second frost hit the Brazilian crop, the cumulative effects destroying about 40% of the coffee. The price of green coffee rose by 330% in three months. Eventually Starbucks had to raise their prices but only by 10%, reflecting only the actual cost increases for that fiscal year. Concern about whether customer demand would drop in the end proved unfounded. The short-term problem was over. Starbucks' customers were prepared to pay a little extra for a quality product. The company made the decision to continue buying stocks, reasoning that it was better to have product at any price than to run out. This caused some financial problems, as some of the buying was at the very peak of the coffee price rise, and retail prices had to be increased again. However the strategy was the right one. Customers could still be supplied.

It has made sense for Starbucks to branch out to a degree, given this dependence on one product. The Tazo® operation, started in 1996, aims to do for tea what Starbucks has done for coffee. Tea is supplied to restaurants, specialist outlets and of course the Starbucks chain.

The music one hears at Starbucks' stores comes from Hear Music, a Starbucks company that not only operates within Starbucks' stores but also has its own stores and Website. There is even a relationship with the *New York Times*: the national newspaper is sold at Starbucks' US locations with the paper using its resources to advertise Starbucks.

In July 2001, Starbucks announced its third quarter results with an anticipated 25% growth in total revenues in the 2002 fiscal year. In that same period it is the intention to open 1200 new stores and start a loyalty card scheme.

By the end of the 2005 fiscal year Starbucks intends to have more than 10,000 stores and a revenue of $6.6bn.

Coffee may be a mundane product, but for generations it has been associated with social intercourse and business. The insurance operation of Lloyds started in a London coffee shop. What Starbucks has done is to bring this experience to a wider audience in a modern setting.

KEY LEARNING POINTS

» Those planning to grow by expanding into a more global market should do so carefully and in incremental steps.
» The Starbucks strategy of simultaneous growth at home and abroad has much to commend it, as it provides for a local fallback position.

» Business may be conducted very differently in other countries and this may cause a conflict with rules and legislation in the company's home country.

» Organizations planning to expand beyond their home borders must always take into account cultural differences.

State-of-the-Art

Management of Growth

» Organizations can grow either organically or by mergers and acquisitions.

» Organic growth may occur by portfolio expansion, horizontal diversification, vertical diversification, or a mixture of all three.

» Alliances and franchising are less risky means of achieving organizational growth.

» Growth should be in line with the organization's mission and vision.

» Growing organizations need to prepare a business plan.

» Organizational and external analysis allow the organization to identify opportunities and threats that will affect growth.

» Successful growth depends upon the control and monitoring of resources and finance.

» Effective communication is an important factor in managing growth.

» People are the most critical aspect of the growth process. Growth often involves expanding the staff numbers.

» Organizational structures and systems may have to change as the organization grows.

» Growth involves changes in organizational culture as well as the more tangible aspects of organizational design.

The companies that appear in the next chapter as case studies – Wal-Mart, Dixons Group, and Hyundai – have made managing growth seem, on the face of it, an easy thing to do. Those in business, however, know that in terms of growth, appearances can be deceptive. What may appear to be linear growth may in fact be one step forward and two steps back.

Growth is something that all organizations, whether they are operating for profit in the private sector or are in the public domain of operations, can achieve. The material in this chapter is designed to provide you with an appreciation of the factors that need to be considered when managing the growth process.

HOW ORGANIZATIONS CAN GROW

There are a number of methods for organizations to grow, either by expanding themselves (organic growth), by partnerships and alliances, or by mergers and acquisitions. It is, of course, possible to combine these methods.

Organic growth

Growth from within an organization can result from expansion within its current market and product portfolio or from attempts to diversify. The major problem with remaining in the same trading position and merely expanding the customer base is that this can limit opportunities. The company may attract new customers that are located further away, but logistics then become a problem. Most organizations growing organically do so through diversification.

There are three main methods of diversifying organically:

» Expanding the portfolio
» Horizontal diversification
» Vertical diversification.

Expanding the portfolio often involves developing a family of products or services. Much of the success that the major car manufacturers enjoy results from the "families" of models that they offer their customers. This allows the customer to either choose the equipment level of a certain model to suit the amount they are prepared to pay, or to trade up to a more expensive model made by that manufacturer. The importance of this portfolio family is that it keeps the customer with the organization as his or her needs change.

Often adding a new model can allow the organization to appeal to a new customer base. By introducing the Neon and the PT Cruiser to their European market in addition to the large four-wheel drive vehicles previously available in Europe, Chrysler has been able to gain a foothold in the lucrative European saloon car market.

Horizontal diversification is growth into related areas. Canon offer printers, scanners, photocopiers, and similar electrical products. The technological link between these is fairly obvious. Together they form part of the equipment used in most offices and increasingly at home. There are advantages (often financial in the form of discounts) in using one supplier for all of one's needs in a particular area.

The growth of supermarket operations (such as that of Wal-Mart as profiled in Chapter 7) is an example of horizontal diversification. This has been a method of growth for a considerable period of retail history as new lines are added to the stock offered. The expansion into groceries, consumer electronics, cleaning services, and even banking is a natural method of growth for the supermarket operators. The advantage to the customer, the USP (Unique Selling Point), is that everything is conveniently under one roof.

Vertical diversification occurs when the organization grows by developing or acquiring other parts of the supply chain. Thomson, the UK package holiday giant, started with the sale of holiday packages. The next move was into charter airline operations (Britannia Airways), thus allowing Thomson considerable flexibility in transporting their customers to their destinations. In the 1990s, Thomson began to operate cruise ships under their own brand. Similar moves into airline and cruise operations have been made by the other two large UK package vacation operators, Airtours and First Choice. Disney, originally a movie-making operation, then developed theme parks, with the attractions based on Disney characters. Then came hotels to service the accommodation needs of those visiting the parks. The latest Disney diversification has also been into the cruise industry, the company operating two large modern vessels in conjunction with theme park vacations.

Alliances and franchising

Alliances are formed when the parties concerned recognize that they can achieve better results in conjunction with another organization than on their own. Nominally the parties remain independent, but that independence can be – and often is – threatened if one or more of the partners have far more power and influence than the others. An alliance between a supplier and a major customer may lead to the supplier becoming totally dependent on that customer.

For example, in 1999 there was considerable concern that the Rover car plant in the UK Midlands would be closed down by its owners, the German giant BMW. Not only would this have led to job losses and hardships among the plant's workers but effects would also have been felt by those in the many suppliers to Rover in the area, so dependent were they on the Rover business.

Franchising is a useful way for an organization with a highly marketable product or service to grow relatively painlessly and at little risk. By selling franchises in return for the use of its name, management expertise, and training etc., the franchisor can expand its market penetration and the franchisee can start his or her own business with the support of a larger organization behind him or her. McDonald's is probably the best-known franchise in the world. British Airways has also franchised its name to local airlines, who could then operate using aircraft in BA liveries and with the crew in BA uniforms. This made it appear that they were actually part of a huge international airline. Sam Walton of Wal-Mart started as a franchisee (see Chapter 7) and his company is now a huge, global retail operation.

Mergers and acquisitions

The simplest way to grow quickly is to *acquire* an organization already operating in a particular market. Being acquired can also lead to growth. As Anslinger and Copeland (quoted earlier) have shown, this can be a very effective way of achieving growth quickly. The acquisition of Sunglass Hut by Desai Capital in 1988 led to Sunglass Hut growing from less than 200 outlets in the US to over 800 throughout the world and a 37% return on investment – over double the figure usually expected. Both the acquirer and acquiree can benefit from each other. The former gains market entry and the later often requires capital to fund its desired growth.

Entrepreneurs are often willing to sell their creations once they have established a market presence. The true entrepreneur, once his or her idea is realised, usually wishes to move on to a new challenge, so the sale of a creation is not as traumatic as might be imagined.

Not all acquisitions are welcome and governments usually have policies on mergers and acquisitions to prevent a monopoly situation developing. However, for organizations that wish to grow and have the finance to acquire others, acquiring an established operator provides a means of entering a market and hopefully retaining the customer base that the acquired organization has built up.

Mergers tend to be more of an agreement between equals than a purchase by one of the other. They are often undertaken to exploit synergy and provide the means by which both organizations can effectively double in size by combining resources.

There are considerable advantages to becoming bigger, not least of which is the ability to buy using economies of scale and to rationalize managerial and logistical operations to cut overall costs. There is little point in doubling in size or revenue if costs increase more than two-fold.

MISSION AND VISION

The issuing of a mission statement is common practice for contemporary organizations. Many mission statements are just bland wish-lists, but they should reflect the vision that is moving the organization forward. Vision and growth need to be linked. Growth should be in line with the vision of those responsible for the management of the organization.

Growth is often most easily managed when it provides synergy with other parts of the organization's operations. In their book *In Search of Excellence*, Peters and Waterman referred to this as "sticking to the knitting." Organizations often operate most effectively in areas they know about. Anslinger and Copeland have challenged the synergy approach. Writing in *Strategies for Growth* (a Harvard Business Review book), they comment that organizations that are prepared to put in considerable effort can diversify into totally new fields and can bring fresh ideas to the marketplace – it does take effort, however.

Non-synergical growth is often harder to align with the vision and mission of the organization. One way around this, often employed, is to keep the growth separate and run distinct organizations that are used to feed funds into the parent company.

Whenever there is a merger or acquisition there will need to be a further refinement of the vision and mission of the organization to accommodate the new partners in the venture. This can be a difficult time as managers, employees, suppliers, and customers become accustomed to a new set of organizational dynamics.

THE BUSINESS PLAN

Whatever methods an organization uses to expand, it will need a business plan. Philip Walcoff makes the point in his *Business Planning for Growth* that a proper plan is a prerequisite for successful growth. A business plan will provide a focus for growth. Unfocused growth is nearly always transitory as it lacks direction.

It is a military maxim that no plan ever survives the first encounter with the enemy. Plans are not static documents but dynamic pointers to a direction. Plans that are adhered to slavishly without regard to the external environment are probably as bad as no plans at all. The plan is the first step along the road of growth. Thereafter it should be monitored and changed as necessary.

A plan also allows the organization to show others – investors, bankers, etc. – how it intends to grow, the steps that will be taken, and the resources needed. There is nothing like putting a plan down in writing to help clarify the mind.

A good business plan will address the financial issues, especially that of cashflow, and help ensure that the organization does not over-reach itself by trying to grow so quickly that it runs out of ready cash. This is an ever-present danger for growing organizations. The plant and materials required to fill orders often have to be paid for well in advance of any associated revenue, and the larger the growth the higher the organization's exposure and the more it may need to borrow to cover the gap.

Business plans are not solely the preserve of senior managers. The more that other people in the organization know about the plan (whilst retaining sensitive commercial information), the more they can see how they fit into that plan and the future growth of the organization. The importance of people to the growth process is covered later in this material, but it can be stated here that the more a person knows and understands, the more that person will be able to contribute to organizational growth.

ANALYSIS

As part of the planning process it is vital that the organization has an ongoing process of analyzing both the internal and external environments.

The organization needs to know what is happening in the outside world, especially in the key PESTLE areas i.e.

» **P**olitical
» **E**conomic
» **S**ocial
» **T**echnological
» **L**egal
» **E**nvironmental.

It is an analysis of these factors that will provide an indication of the opportunities for growth and the threats that might confront the organization.

These are then fed into a SWOT analysis:

» **S**trength
» **W**eaknesses
» **O**pportunities
» **T**hreats.

The strengths and weaknesses are internal to the organization, whereas the opportunities and threats are derived from the PESTLE analysis.

This type of analysis should be conducted on an ongoing basis as the environment in which the organization operates is likely to be subject to change itself.

RESOURCES AND FINANCE

One of the biggest problems in managing growth is the acquisition of resources. Growth can either consume resources at a faster rate than the organization can replenish them or it can cause the organization to be caught unawares and suffer a stock-out situation.

Of all the critical resources needed for growth, money is possibly the most important. Running out of money is a disaster for any organization. As has already been mentioned, it is important that there is sufficient money in place to finance growth. It may be some time before the growth produces revenue and in that time the very act of growing may be eating into the organization's cash reserves. Banks are normally more than happy to fund growth, especially when it is backed by a properly worked out business plan. However borrowed money has to be repaid with interest. Suppliers will not want to wait for payment and employee and overhead costs have to be met. Growth may involve investment in new plant. Thus the costs of growth may be fairly substantial in the short term and it is for the organization to make an informed decision as to whether the potential gains are worth these costs. Sometimes it is better to turn work away if taking an order requires considerable investment. If the order is likely to be repeated then the investment will pay off but if it is not repeated then the organization could become stuck with under-utilized plant and a surfeit of stock.

CUSTOMERS

Customers are key to growth. Growth can either follow the increase in customer demand or the organization may try to stimulate demand and, in effect, *create* a market. The latter strategy can be a risky one. In 2000 it was considered that there would be a considerable growth in the sales of WAP mobile telephones in the UK. However, it appeared that the customer base was not yet ready for such a move and sales were much lower than anticipated. Perhaps one of the classic examples of trying to create a demand was the Ford Edsel of the 1950s. Considered by its designers to be the latest in state-of-the-art automobile design and manufacture, the vehicle did not sell. Indeed it was only in the 1990s that it became desirable – as a collector's item. Unfortunately insufficient customer research had been carried out.

There is often a considerable difference between what customers say that they will pay for and what they will actually hand over money for when it is available.

Market research is a specialized field and most organizations regard the purchase of high quality market research as an investment. Nevertheless, the cautionary note is that the only true way of knowing whether a product or service will be a success is when people actually go out and acquire it.

Repeat business

Customers (whatever they are called – clients, patients, passengers, etc.) are the most important people with whom an organization has a relationship. No customers eventually means no business. It is customers who pay the wages.

One of the best business performance indicators is that of repeat business – do customers come back? Repeat customers are often a useful source of market research. Their views should be listened to as they may well be the people who will assist in the growth process.

There are some areas of business that do not necessarily *want* repeat customers, for example law enforcement and medical services, but in the main these are areas where society does not really want growth. They are the grudge purchases as covered below.

Grudge purchases

Grudge purchases are those things that everybody knows they need but resents paying for. Insurance, dentists, funerals, law enforcement – even politicians and government. Organizations seeking to grow in these areas need to adopt a tactic of stressing benefits rather than products. In recent years, in various countries there has been a growth in pre-paid funeral packages. Paying in advance for one's own funeral is perhaps the ultimate in grudge purchases. It is testimony to the skills of those in the industry that it has been possible to stress the benefits so as to create a growth opportunity in this field of enterprise.

COMMUNICATION

There is no point in having a concept that will grab the imagination of customers and lead to growth if it cannot be communicated to them. Communication, either informally or formally as part of advertising, is an important aspect of the growth process and should form part of the business plan.

One problem that may occur is stimulating the market for competitors by raising customer awareness. Customer behavior often follows a pattern known as AIDA:

» **Attention**
» **Interest**
» **Desire**
» **Action.**

In order to attract the customer's *attention*, he or she has to know about you and your products. This may be through advertising but it may also be through conversation with friends and colleagues. Advertising, by its very nature, is in the public domain and is thus available to competitors. Hopefully effective advertising will increase either the size of the customer base or the quantity of current customer uptake – both leading to growth. Once *attention* has been gained then, if the customer feels that the product or service is right for them, their *interest* is stirred. Once somebody is interested they will try to find out more about what is on offer. If they still like what they see and hear, they will begin to *desire* the product or service and that will produce *action* to acquire it for themselves or their client.

From the growth and competition viewpoints there are two major problems associated with AIDA:

» Stimulating demand for one product, service, or even supplier tends to stimulate demand for similar offerings across the market. An effective advertising campaign for one brand of coffee tends to produce increases in sales for all coffee manufacturers. Provided that the company is providing a good level of product and customer service this will not be too much of a problem, but it will not want to stimulate interest in its competitors. Once the company has gained attention and interest, the customer is likely to purchase, so the company must make sure that it, and not a competitor, gains the purchase. At the start of the home computer boom in the 1980s, Sinclair Electronics stimulated massive interest with their relatively cheap machines. Unfortunately they could not supply enough of them and purchasers had to go elsewhere and once there, they stayed with the competition, to the detriment and downfall of Sinclair.

» It is very easy to lose a purchase at any stage. If, having gained attention, the company is unable to fulfil the customer's need for information in the interest stage; it risks losing him or her altogether. Bad service at any stage after gaining attention can mean a lost customer on a permanent basis. Every expression of interest should be treated as potential desire and eventual action. The aim is to ensure that the action is with the company, thus producing growth, and not with a competitor. Desire without fulfilment can fade quickly. This is known in the US as "buyer's regret." Once the customer has made up his or her mind, the longer the wait between order and delivery, the greater the danger that the customer will have second thoughts.

There is a complementary title in the *ExpressExec* series – *Communication* – which covers the whole subject of communication in more depth.

PEOPLE

Next to customers, employees are the most important people to an organization. Without motivated employees, growth will be at best difficult and at worst impossible.

Motivation and momentum

The momentum for growth eventually depends on the motivation of the people involved. The more employees feel involved, the more they will be motivated to assist the organization in growing. Organizations that do not look after their people may grow in the short term but over the medium to long term often find that those individuals who have contributed most to growth have left to work for others. If they have moved to a competitor then the organization has a real problem, as its best growth agents are now working against it.

Growth is not always a straight-line linear process. Even with the best will in the world there are likely to be setbacks. Keeping motivation and momentum high is crucial at these times. The more people are informed the more likely they are to work together to overcome difficulties.

New people

Growth often means the recruitment of new staff. Initially these may be temporary hires hoping that the positions will become permanent. The integration of new hires with established staff should be handled sensitively, especially if the growth is creating a need for a large expansion in staff numbers. New employees may feel intimidated by those who have been with the organization some time and they in turn may feel threatened by newcomers.

A good plan is to use established people to assist with the induction and training of newcomers – this is likely to promote teamwork. If such a growth in staff is not handled sensitively, motivation and thus productivity can suffer. It is especially important to be sensitive after a merger or acquisition where the aim should be to create an integrated workforce not a "them and us" situation.

What to do with those who cannot cope

It is in the nature of any form of change, however desirable it might be, that there will be those who cannot cope with it. People become very comfortable in their ways and may find that the sudden impetus of growth is difficult for them to cope with.

If somebody has given their energy and loyalty to an organization it may well be worth trying to find an area of the growing company in which they can still make a contribution. Such people are often of considerable use in roles such as training new staff, special projects, and customer relations.

It may well be that some people take longer to come to terms with the new form of the organization. It is worth remembering that once somebody leaves a company their knowledge, skills, special expertise, and contacts tend to leave with them and become lost to the organization.

Sometimes hard decisions about people have to be made but it is much better to retain expertise within the organization whenever possible. If, however, people cannot really cope and have to leave, sensitivity and dignity should be considered. It is always worth remembering that every employee may also be a potential customer.

ORGANIZATION STRUCTURE

It is a feature of organizational growth that the structure of the organization needs to change as it becomes larger.

The structure of small organizations may be very simple indeed – one person in charge and a small number of employees. Communication tends to be direct and immediate – everybody can talk to everybody else face to face. This simplicity and the effectiveness that goes with it may not be possible as the organization grows and the gap between those at the top of a developing hierarchy and those further down becomes larger.

Span of control

As organizations became larger during the industrial revolution (see Chapter 3), business organizations began to discover a fact that had been known to military commanders for centuries. There is a limit to the number of people that can be effectively supervised by a single individual. Armies, for time immemorial, have been arranged in sub-platoons, platoons, regiments, brigades, and so on, and these are led by increasingly higher-ranking individuals. The number that can be supervised by one person is somewhere around ten – not a large number. Just like military formations, organizations have developed supervisory/managerial structures based on this "span of control."

The growing organization needs to address the setting up or adaptation of existing supervisory/managerial structures. As the organization moves into a multi-site operation so it will be necessary to clarify the relationships between the central headquarters' function and those of the various sites. Such matters should be given careful consideration. The relationships are very important to the success of the growth process. The correct degree of autonomy needs to be given to managers to allow them to make decisions. Peters and Waterman have described the importance of what they termed simultaneous loose–tight properties, where the headquarters keeps a tight rein on the vision and financial control whilst allowing managers to make decisions as close to the point of the customer interface as possible.

Organizational structures should be designed around the needs of the customers and processes. There is no right or wrong way to structure an organization – it is a case of what works best in the particular circumstances. Structures that are useful in a growth phase and allow for rapid changes may be less suitable for more stable times.

SYSTEMS

As with structures, the systems used by an organization as it grows are likely to change. Technology, as shown in Chapter 4, has revolutionized communication. A growing organization may well need ever more sophisticated communication, control, and monitoring systems. It will take time for people to become used to these changes. Training needs should never be neglected if maximum return is to be gained from the investment of the systems needed to support growth.

Growing organizations may well not possess in-house the necessary technical expertise for developing the necessary systems. Development can be outsourced but it is necessary to remember that the systems need to fit the organization's need and not be what suits those developing them. New systems need to be debugged. Nothing annoys customers and suppliers more than being told that an error is due to a systems failure! Systems should be debugged before they are put into the public domain.

CULTURE

Culture, the "way things are done around here," can vary considerably between small and large organizations. The former may be informal and centered on just one person – the owner/founder. Large organizations are often quite bureaucratic. Cultural changes are amongst the slowest there are, often being generational.

Changes in culture can be quite distressing for employees, including the most senior. Cultural changes are often one of the reasons why entrepreneurs sell their creations – it is because the creation appears to be operating in a completely different way from the one they created and thus they set out and create a new business. Culture will change as the organization grows and it is a key task of senior management to ensure that employees know not only what is happening but also why.

MEASURING GROWTH

For organizations with a profit motive, growth can be measured both in financial terms and in the number of employees and customers. Profit, revenue, and return on investment are all financial measures that are employed. A growth in staff employed or even customers is of little use without the likelihood of a rise in profits. Profits may be sacrificed in the short term in order to build up market share. Many Japanese companies used gaining market share by accepting low returns on investment when penetrating the US and European markets. As prices rise once market share has been achieved, profits should be generated. This approach to growth requires investors who are interested in the long-term prospects of the company.

The growth of organizations in the public sector cannot be measured by profit and may be considered in terms of spending, client numbers, or staff size increases.

DECLINE

Whilst this material is about managing growth, there will be times perhaps when an organization needs to become smaller – downsizing was a term much in vogue during the 1990s.

Just as much care needs to be taken when reducing an organization in size. It needs to be accomplished in a planned manner and not appear to be a panic, crisis reaction. The same factors need to be taken into consideration as when managing growth if the organization is going to grow again.

No organization wants to become smaller but external market changes may make it inevitable. Just as growing organizations can be at risk of being acquired by cash-rich predators as funds become necessary to support growth, so a downsizing organization also faces the same risks although for different reasons. In this case funds are required to ensure some form of survival.

KEY LEARNING POINTS

> » There are a number of methods for organizations to grow, which may involve internal organic growth or a process of mergers, acquisitions, alliances, or franchising.

» Growth requires organizational action to change systems, structure, and culture. These changes may make employees uncomfortable.
» Growth is not only about organizations becoming bigger – it has implications for the people involved with the organization.
» Decline needs very similar management to growth.

Growth Management Success Stories

This chapter provides case studies of the following companies.

» Wal-Mart.
» Dixons Group.
» Hyundai.

This chapter uses three case studies to demonstrate how different methods of growth can prove successful. The organizations studied are Wal-Mart, which developed from a regional US supermarket chain to a world-wide hypermarket group; The Dixons Group, originally a London-based photographics store, now the UK's biggest electrical and computer retailer, with several stores abroad; and Hyundai, the Korean automobile manufacturer whose products have become popular across the Western world as well as at home.

CASE 1: WAL-MART

At the end of 1945, Sam Walton, recently discharged from the US army, purchased the franchise on the Butler Brothers store in Newport, Arkansas for $25,000. When Sam Walton died in 1993, *Fortune* magazine reported that his $23.5bn fortune was second only to that of the richest person in the world, the Sultan of Brunei ($37bn).

Today Wal-Mart is a global concern that has spread far beyond its beginnings in Arkansas.

Walton bought other Butler Brothers franchises and was one of the first dry store retailers to introduce the concept of self-service. As his chain of stores grew he learnt to fly so as to save time on the road. In the 1960s many of the controls on prices that had prevented discounting began to be dismantled by State legislatures, and in 1962 Sam Walton opened the first of his very own stores (unconnected with any franchise) in Rogers, Arkansas. The brand name chosen for this new venture was Wal-Mart. As a dry goods operation Wal-Mart was not yet in competition with the supermarkets. The company was incorporated in 1969 and by 1972 it was listed on the NYSE (New York Stock Exchange).

The Wal-Mart chain had grown rapidly but within the confines of Arkansas, Oklahoma, and Missouri with 11, 2, and 5 stores respectively.

Wal-Mart focused on low prices and basic facilities. The stores operated a 12-hour day from 9.00 am, six days per week. Sunday was sacrosanct in the early days. Each store was located on a prime site as Walton was well aware that location, location, location can make or break a retailing operation.

As time went on the stores became bigger and air-conditioning was introduced together with ever larger parking lots. The company was an early acceptor of credit card purchases. In 1969 these accounted for just 3% of the total purchases in the US. The days of using credit/charge cards for everyday purchases was yet to come but by accepting them Wal-Mart showed its customers that it was moving into a new era of retailing. Walton, while primarily interested in his Wal-Mart discount operation, still had a chain of 14 variety stores from his previous enterprises but, by 1970, over 70% of the income was derived from Wal-Mart. By then the corporate headquarters was at a new railroad-connected facility in Bentonville. The railroad connection was important for Bentonville's role as a distribution center.

By 1970 Wal-Mart was recording annual sales in excess of $30mn.

By 1975 the Wal-Mart chain had increased to 100 city discount stores plus two each of the Save-Co Building Supply and Home Improvement Centers and Family Center variety stores located over eight States. In 1975 Wal-Mart acquired three Howard Discount Centers and the following year the this was supplemented by 16 Mohr-Value stores in Michigan and Illinois. Growth was now a twin-track affair of expansion organically and by acquisition.

Horizontal diversification occurred in 1978 with the opening of pharmacy, jewelry, and auto-service within the stores, plus the acquisition of the Hutcheson Shoe Company. The Wal-Mart growth philosophy at the time was to target those towns that were being ignored by other retailers. By 1979 sales had topped the billion-dollar mark. Acquisitions continued, with US Woolco being bought in 1983 – the year the "people greeter" concept was implemented across all Wal-Mart locations and one-hour photographic laboratories were introduced.

Up to this time Wal-Mart had been concentrated in the South and Midwest of the US, still appearing very much as a regional operator. In the late 1980s, however, the organization began to expand throughout the US. The opening of warehouse clubs that also sold packaged groceries in urban areas was a major diversification from the dry goods market. These were soon to be called Sam's Clubs. By 1991, the year after Wal-Mart became the number one retailer in the US, there were no fewer than 148 Sam's Clubs in nearly half of the States of the Union.

Hypermarkets, a blend of supermarket food operations and discount dry goods, had been developing in Europe since the 1960s. Walton decided that the time was ripe to extend this "one-stop shop" concept to the US. That Wal-Mart was doing well was amply illustrated by the fact that, whereas in 1979 annual sales were $1bn, during the December 1993 run up to Christmas and New Year Wal-Mart recorded its first $1bn week.

The US was no longer big enough for Wal-Mart. The company entered Mexico in 1991, Canada – through the purchase of Woolco's Canadian operation – in 1994, Argentina and Brazil in 1995, and the potentially huge Chinese market in 1996.

Wal-Mart staff had been known as "associates" from the earliest days and in 1997 the company became the largest employer in the US, having grown to 680,000 US associates in addition to another 115,000 abroad.

The German organization Weftkauf was acquired in 1997, giving Wal-Mart a European foothold that was to be strengthened in 1999 when it acquired the ASDA Group and its 229 stores in the UK. ASDA (as Associated Dairies) had been a founder and major player in the UK supermarket business, together with Tesco, Sainsbury's, and Somerfield. Bill Quinn (no lover of Wal-Mart) has described this as a "Wal-Mart invasion of Britain."

Quinn is highly critical of Wal-Mart's expansion, as shown by his book *How Wal-Mart is Destroying America (and the World) and What You Can Do About It*. However, it is a fact that consumers want discounted products. In 1999 Wal-Mart was ranked as Number One Corporate Citizen in the US, seventh in *Fortune* magazine's "most admired companies in the world," and sixth in overall corporate reputation in the US, according to Interactive Inc.

Modern hypermarkets may, as Quinn points out, destroy the business of local retailers but they are what customers want. Wal-Mart should not be blamed for responding to demand. In building large out-of-town facilities in the UK, Wal-Mart (through ASDA) are following the pattern laid out by Tesco.

Wal-Mart has entered Korea and further expansion seems likely. The pattern of growth for Wal-Mart and other similar operations has been one of horizontal diversification to expand the portfolio of goods and services available and acquisitions to gain market penetration.

In 1998 Wal-Mart's annual charitable contributions totaled $102mn, the company having made a $551mn operating profit the previous year.

Whether one admires Sam Walton's creation or not (and there is much to be said for the service levels of local, smaller retailers), the discounted prices of the hypermarkets have brought a wider range of goods within the reach of more people.

Wal-Mart is probably one of the best examples of how to manage growth by using a variety of means and as such deserves a place in this material.

A timeline for Wal-Mart is provided in Fig. 7.1.

WAL-MART: KEY INSIGHTS

» Growth has been by diversification, geographic expansion from the home base, and acquisition.

» Diversification by Wal-Mart has been in steps that supplement the core operation, e.g. the introduction of a pharmacy operation into stores.

» Wal-Mart has not been afraid to copy ideas, such as the European hypermarket concept.

» Walton started as a franchisee and then set up his own operation.

» Foreign expansion has been logical – North America then South America; Germany then UK, etc.

» Wal-Mart listens to the customer, understands what he or she wants, and then provides it.

CASE 2: DIXONS GROUP

In 1937 Charles Kalms opened the first Dixons photographic studio in Southend, a popular UK holiday resort for Londoners. Despite the unsettled international situation this was a highly propitious move as throughout the war years there was an unprecedented demand for portrait photography, particularly from service personnel and their families. The company flourished and during the war set up seven studios in the London area. But in 1945 the market contracted as dramatically as it had expanded and the company was reduced to a single studio in Edgware, a north London suburb.

Whilst the war was a devastating experience for millions, at its conclusion there were large numbers of people who had received

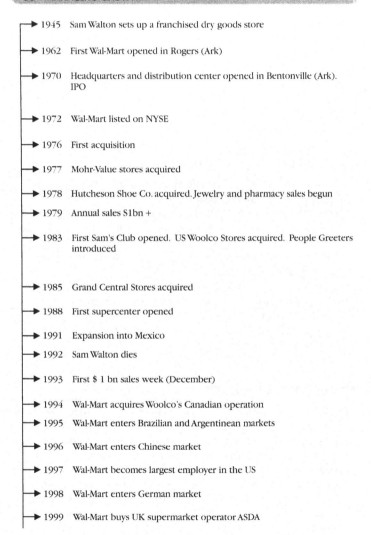

1945	Sam Walton sets up a franchised dry goods store
1962	First Wal-Mart opened in Rogers (Ark)
1970	Headquarters and distribution center opened in Bentonville (Ark). IPO
1972	Wal-Mart listed on NYSE
1976	First acquisition
1977	Mohr-Value stores acquired
1978	Hutcheson Shoe Co. acquired. Jewelry and pharmacy sales begun
1979	Annual sales $1bn +
1983	First Sam's Club opened. US Woolco Stores acquired. People Greeters introduced
1985	Grand Central Stores acquired
1988	First supercenter opened
1991	Expansion into Mexico
1992	Sam Walton dies
1993	First $ 1 bn sales week (December)
1994	Wal-Mart acquires Woolco's Canadian operation
1995	Wal-Mart enters Brazilian and Argentinean markets
1996	Wal-Mart enters Chinese market
1997	Wal-Mart becomes largest employer in the US
1998	Wal-Mart enters German market
1999	Wal-Mart buys UK supermarket operator ASDA

Fig. 7.1 Timeline of growth of Wal-Mart.

new experiences. Millions had learnt to drive, others had flown – these were to create new markets. Stanley Kalms, Charles' son, was quick to recognize the public's new-found interest in photography that had started during the war and was now growing rapidly.

He persuaded his father to sell the simple cameras that were coming on to the market and the accessories to go with them. The idea of a family holiday was now firmly part of both the working- and middle-class tradition and taking a camera to record such events was something everybody could now do.

The Kalms advertised new and second-hand photographic products in trade, local and national press. This marketing approach quickly laid the foundations for a mail order division which, coupled with customer-friendly credit agreements, ensured Dixons entered the 1950s as the number one photographic dealer in the UK. This market leadership was maintained and developed throughout the 1950s by offering competitively priced products with quality service.

By 1957 Dixons had expanded so rapidly that it was forced to find a new head office to accommodate the growing number of employees dealing with 60,000 mail order customers, and to provide administrative backup for the six stores it had opened. Soon the office in Edgware became a buying center as Stanley Kalms started regular trips to the Far East to purchase items from the rapidly growing photographic manufacturing operations in the region. He forged vital links with Japanese manufacturers who supplied Dixons directly with products often made to the company's own specification and sold under the brand name of Prinz – a procedure now known as generic branding and pioneered by retailers such as Sears in the US.

Hard bargaining and bulk buying, predominantly in Japan, gave Dixons the competitive edge over its UK rivals, especially as the quality of Japanese products soon rose to match those of traditional US and European manufacturers.

Dixons, having expanded to 16 branches, made its IPO on the London Stock Exchange under the name of Dixons Photographic Limited in 1962. A rapid expansion of the store portfolio followed throughout the 1960s, including the acquisition of major competitors Ascotts (1962) and Bennetts (1964), which added 42 retail outlets to the Dixons chain. Like many organizations, Dixons expanded by acquisition at this time and has continued to do so both in the UK and abroad, as will be shown later. As covered in Chapters 3 and 6, acquisitions and mergers are a useful means of expansion, bringing with them as they do both premises and a customer base.

Having been involved in selling cameras and photographic equipment in 1967 Dixons diversified into developing and printing by taking control of a color processing laboratory in Stevenage, the most up-to-date in Europe at the time. Again mail order on a massive scale became key to the company's success.

Consumer electronics as an adjunct to the photographic side came with the introduction of Japanese audio and hi-fi units into the Dixons range.

Charles Kalms retired as chairman in 1971 and was succeeded by his son Stanley. Charles then became life president of the Group.

The 15 shops owned by Wallace Heaton in the London area were acquired in 1972. The gradual reduction in the working week meant more leisure time for everyone. A number of Dixons stores included sports departments and photography as a hobby boomed, increasing sales of cameras (of increasing sophistication) year on year throughout the decade.

In 1974 Dixons opened its main Stevenage Distribution Center on a seven-acre site with computerized control and conveyor belt stock handling. At the time this was the largest computerized warehouse in Europe.

Charles Kalms died at the age of 80 in 1978 having seen his Southend venture of 1937 develop into a major UK retailing chain.

Dixons introduced Saisho own-brand products in 1982. The use of a Far Eastern brand name provided a high technology image, with the brand including audio, TV, and video products – the growing "brown goods" market that was being fuelled by increased leisure time and higher disposable incomes.

A major acquisition in 1984 was the UK Currys Group, adding 613 retail outlets to the Dixons organization together with Mastercare, the nationwide electrical appliance service organization with 41 depots and 900 engineers. Also part of the deal was Bridgers, a chain of white and brown goods discount stores that formed the basis of today's Currys Superstores, bringing Dixons into the refrigerator, washing machine, and cooking appliance markets. Other subsequent acquisitions have included a number of similar chains, such as Orbit and Greens. Many customers seem unaware that Dixons and Currys are part of the same group. In 1996 when this writer and his colleague George Green were researching for a text on customer satisfaction they met a lady who had bought a Saisho tape recorder/radio at Dixons but had later found a much "nicer" (her words) one from Currys and "it had colored buttons and was much better value". The machines were identical (except for the buttons) and actually the same price!

The Group acquired the Supasnaps chain of 337 specialist photo shops in 1986, a reversion to the original business. The next year (1987 – the Group's fiftieth anniversary) saw a major development with the acquisition of Silo, the US's third largest power retailer with 147 stores. Dixons was expanding out of the UK into the global market.

The acquisition of Wigfalls (based in the Midlands and Northern England) in 1988 brought another 106 outlets into the Group. Many of Dixons and Currys head office departments and support functions were integrated into a single entity in that year, Dixons Stores Group. The two chains, however, retained their own marketing identity and continue to do so, often being sited quite near to each other with most UK towns having both a Dixons and a Currys store.

The film processing division was sold to its management in 1989, a rationalization that reflected the retail nature of the Dixons organization. Growth sometimes involves contraction as well as expansion, as covered in Chapter 6.

Whilst Dixons had been an early entrant into the home computer market, a major expansion in computer retailing occurred in 1993 with the acquisition of the Vision Technology Group (VTG), a company operating four PC World Superstores and which had acquired a group of companies engaged in the sale by mail order of personal computers, peripherals, software, and accessories to companies, educational institutions, and private individuals.

In November 1991, VTG had opened the first PC World Superstore in Croydon, specializing in the sale of personal computers and related products. The next year it had opened a second Superstore on the Lakeside Retail Park at West Thurrock, and then more stores in Brentford and Staples Corner. All of these outlets were in the London area.

After its acquisition by Dixons Group, VTG's mail order division was sold off to enable the Group to focus on the retail side of the business. The Group also sold Dixons US Holdings Inc, Silo's parent company, to Fretter Inc, in which it retained a 30% stake.

Supasnaps was sold to Sketchley plc, a company perhaps better known for their dry cleaning operations.

In 1994 Dixons Group announced the pilot of a new shopping format called The Link, which would sell the latest generation of communication services and products thus taking advantage of the growth in mobile telephone usage in the UK, usage that was to grow almost exponentially throughout the rest of the decade to the point where 50% of the population were mobile telephone users and owners by 2000.

The first Dixons tax-free store opened at Heathrow's Terminal 3 on July 18, 1994. Retail is a major part of airport operations in the UK and the airport authorities and the retailers have realized that waiting outbound passengers are a captive market looking for something to do to pass the time – what better than discount shopping. Despite European Union (EU) restrictions on duty free sales for travelers within the EU, airports such as Heathrow cater for many long-haul passengers and thus bargains can still be obtained.

In December of 1994, the Group moved its head office to new premises in Hemel Hempstead, Hertfordshire.

The Group opened the largest electrical superstore in Europe in 1995, the Currys Superstore at Junction 9 of the M6 Motorway (Freeway) in Birmingham. It also opened the fourth Dixons tax-free shop at Heathrow's Terminal 4, following the success of its other tax-free shops at Heathrow and London's Gatwick airport.

PC World's portfolio also expanded with further openings in a number of principal towns and cities in the UK, the PC World operation becoming national rather than regional in character. Many of the sites are in the new out-of-town shopping malls that have been developed in the UK along the US model. It is rare to find one of these that does not include one of the Dixons Group outlets and frequently there may be more than one – a Dixons and a Currys being not unusual.

Group chairman Stanley Kalms was awarded a knighthood by Her Majesty the Queen in the New Year's Honors List in 1996 in recognition of his services to electrical retailing. In April of that year,

Dixons stores became the first to sell the new Advanced Photographic System (APS) cameras. In November, the Group acquired DN Computer Services plc (DNCS), the computer reseller business, which formed part of the PC World division. DNCS enabled PC World to establish an even stronger position in the £3bn business-to-business market, thus expanding Dixons Group activities from the domestic to the business sector. A £20mn expansion plan for the Stevenage Distribution Center was announced which, when completed in August 1997, doubled its capacity. In December, the Group opened its first store in the Republic of Ireland, launching a £10mn investment in the Irish market over three years which had created 300 job opportunities by the end of 1998.

The expansion into the Republic of Ireland continued in 1997 when Dixons Group acquired the retail assets of Harry Moore Ltd., the Ireland-based electrical retailer and specialist in TV rental, finance, and mobile communications. Meanwhile a third Dixons store opened in Dublin.

Telecom Securicor Cellular Radio Limited (Cellnet) bought a 40% stake in The Link, Dixons' specialist mobile phone and communications retailer.

In July, the Group announced record profits of £190.2mn and its intention to create 3000 jobs over the next financial year.

In September, the Group launched PC World Business Direct, a new IT mail order service incorporating the brand strength of PC World and the sector expertise of DNCS.

The UK's apparent £8bn a year obsession with electronic gadgetry was marked in October with the official launch of Dixons Online as the first UK electrical goods Internet home-shopping service. Customers were offered guaranteed next-day delivery of over 2000 products within the mainland UK. Details of this and other Dixons operations can be found via their Website, the address of which is given in Chapter 9.

The Group strengthened its presence in Ireland in November of 1997, opening the first PC World store (and largest computer superstore) in the Republic. One advantage of operating in the Republic of Ireland is that the electricity supply system is the same as the UK and there are no language problems with instructions etc.

The Group acquired Byte Computer Superstores Ltd. with 16 retail outlets in 1998 and assisted the UK government's New Deal scheme to reduce youth unemployment by announcing plans to take on a further

100 employees from the scheme. In July, the Group took on its first New Deal trainee in Scotland.

During the same month, the Group also announced pre-tax profits of £217.6mn and plans to open more than 100 new stores in 1998/99 creating around 2000 additional jobs – a useful boost to the UK economy.

Currys became the first electrical retailer to stock plasma flat TVs in widescreen format. Later in the year, Currys and Dixons were among the first retailers to sell integrated digital TVs.

In September, the Group launched Freeserve, the UK's first fully featured Internet service provider (ISP) available free with no registration or subscription fees. It also announced the trial of a new retail/e-tail concept called @jakarta, dedicated to selling software and games.

In January 1999, chief executive John Clare announced changes to the Group's corporate structure to build on its success and create a new framework for growth. Dixons Group Retail Properties Limited was established to manage and develop the Group's retail portfolio.

The Link sold its millionth mobile phone after just four years of trading. Freeserve also announced a milestone – its millionth subscriber.

PC World launched a range of furniture for use with PCs and a new online software site with more than 2000 gaming, business, and family titles.

The lowest-priced PC ever offered by a UK retailer – at just £399 – went on sale at PC World, Dixons, and Currys, indicative of just how far PC prices had dropped as a result of the growth in the sector. In June 1999, the Group announced its intention to float 20% of Freeserve, and did so successfully two months later.

In July, the Group announced record pre-tax profits of £237.1mn and plans to create more jobs in the coming year.

Continuing to lead the way in bringing new technology to customers, Dixons Select was launched in October. This shopping channel was launched on Open; the first integrated digital television shopping service. In November, the two hundredth branch of The Link was opened in Glasgow.

In December the group made an offer for the leading Nordic electrical retailer, Elkjøp ASA. Within six weeks the deal was complete and Dixons had thus expanded into Norway, Finland, Iceland, and Sweden.

In January 2000, Dixons Group announced half-year profit before tax of £299.4mn, and a £30mn investment over two years in e-commerce development. The Group also acquired Ei System, the leading specialist PC retailer in Spain and Portugal, to take advantage of the rapidly growing PC market in these countries. This provided Dixons with the six PC City outlets in Spain.

March 2000 saw the opening of a new state-of-the-art customer contact center in Sheffield, creating 2000 new jobs, to handle the increasing number of customer contacts with the Group.

European activity continued in April, when the Group acquired a 15% stake in leading Greek electrical retailer, Kotsovolos, with stores in Greece and the Czech Republic. Kotsovolos also existed as an e-commerce site in France, opening its first store there in 2001.

2000–2001 figures for the Group showed pre-tax profits of £647mn on a turnover of £4688mn.

A strategic partnership was formed with eMachines, a leading supplier of PCs to the US market in August, making Dixons the exclusive supplier of eMachine PCs to third-party retailers in a number of European countries.

Omni Source, a new Group company, was formed later in 2000 to focus on the sourcing of original equipment manufacturer (OEM) products destined for the Group's European retail market.

The Group continued to bring the latest technology to UK customers with the launch of digital radio (the Psion WaveFinder) and TiVo, the intelligent personal video recorder, in its stores in October 2000.

Dixons Group has grown considerably since the original outlet opened in Southend in 1937. However the growth can be seen to have followed a clear and rational pattern from photographic to other brown goods through to computers. The acquisition of companies in the same field added breadth and depth to the Group's activities.

The Group has also been adept at anticipating customer requirements both in terms of products and the type of service required. More leisure time and higher disposable incomes have meant that customers demand higher quality for their products in the areas in which Dixons specializes. The Currys operation dealing in white goods is no longer in a luxury market – washing machines, dryers, refrigerators, etc. are now considered essentials in the UK, as in other developed countries.

They are almost becoming consumables. The setting up of The Link at the very start of the mobile telephone boom gave Dixons a headstart in the market.

If there have been criticisms of the Group, especially the Dixons store operation, they have centered on a lack of product knowledge by the staff. Dixons recognized this and my own recent experiences in seeking information on camcorders and computers suggest that the staff are now very knowledgeable and indeed helpful. One useful way to test customer care strategies is to announce when approached by a salesperson that one has no intention of buying at the moment but needs some information for the future. If the response is still helpful, as it appears to be at Dixons, then the staff have been well trained.

Figure 7.2 shows the Dixons timeline.

DIXONS GROUP: KEY INSIGHTS

» Expansion has been logical.
» Overseas growth occurred after home base had been consolidated.
» Expansion has been mainly achieved by acquisitions bringing with them premises and a customer base.
» Dixons Group has been at the forefront of offering new technology.
» Dixons Group has been a leader in using technology to support traditional sales channels.
» Dixons Group has taken advantage of social and income patterns.

CASE 3: HYUNDAI

Considering the devastation caused by the Korean War in the early 1950s and the prolonged armistice talks, the emergence of a number of large Korean companies expanding into the global marketplace has been testimony to the resilience and work ethic of the people of South Korea.

For much of the twentieth century the Korean peninsular was under the economic/military control of China, Russia, or Japan and it was only

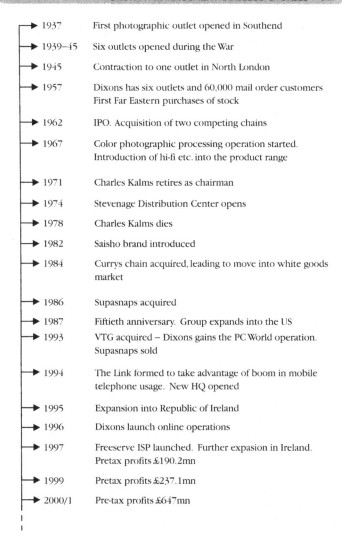

1937	First photographic outlet opened in Southend
1939–45	Six outlets opened during the War
1945	Contraction to one outlet in North London
1957	Dixons has six outlets and 60,000 mail order customers. First Far Eastern purchases of stock
1962	IPO. Acquisition of two competing chains
1967	Color photographic processing operation started. Introduction of hi-fi etc. into the product range
1971	Charles Kalms retires as chairman
1974	Stevenage Distribution Center opens
1978	Charles Kalms dies
1982	Saisho brand introduced
1984	Currys chain acquired, leading to move into white goods market
1986	Supasnaps acquired
1987	Fiftieth anniversary. Group expands into the US
1993	VTG acquired – Dixons gains the PC World operation. Supasnaps sold
1994	The Link formed to take advantage of boom in mobile telephone usage. New HQ opened
1995	Expansion into Republic of Ireland
1996	Dixons launch online operations
1997	Freeserve ISP launched. Further expasion in Ireland. Pretax profits £190.2mn
1999	Pretax profits £237.1mn
2000/1	Pre-tax profits £647mn

Fig. 7.2 Timeline of growth of Dixons Group.

after 1945 that the country of South Korea (that part of the peninsular below the thirty-eighth parallel) was able to develop its own identity.

One of the first purely Korean enterprises was the Hyundai Auto Service Center of 1946, rapidly followed the next year by Hyundai Engineering and Construction.

Hyundai was founded by Chung Ju Yung, who was born in 1915 and who, in October 1998, led the first of 500 cattle across the border with North Korea for delivery to that country's starving peasants – one of the first acts of reconciliation between the two countries since the conflict of the 1950s. Born in what is now North Korea, this was a symbolic journey for Chung Ju Yung, whose Hyundai name was one recognized globally, not least through the automobiles it produced.

The Korean car industry had boomed in the final years of the twentieth century, with 2000 production set to exceed 3.4 mn units. The two major Korean automobile manufacturers, Hyundai and Daewoo, were becoming a threat to the more established global players.

Hyundai's growth had been based on low cost and high quality. A generation earlier, and in common with the perception of Japanese automobiles, the view in Europe and the US had been that the Korean vehicles were basic, cheap, and perhaps a good first automobile for a customer to buy when entering the market. However, like the Japanese, the quality of the Korean vehicles has proved to be high.

Hyundai does not lack ambition. Under its chairman Chung Mong Kyu (Chung Ju Yung's nephew) the target is for 2002 production to reach three million units, with 50% for export. Achieving this would place Hyundai in the global top ten automobile manufacturers.

Hyundai has worked on joint projects with many of the established manufacturers and thus has developed the necessary engineering expertise and the all-important customer knowledge needed for the highly competitive automobile market.

In addition the company has heavy engineering, electrical, and construction operations and thus has diversity in order to ride any economic downturns. The deep Asian economic depression of 1997–98 had a disastrous effect on many Asian businesses and Korea was certainly not immune. Hyundai, however, had announced a $2.3bn investment in the most important emerging market of all – China – and this helped the company weather the storm. The main Korean rival, Daewoo, was not as fortunate. Crippled with a $70bn debt load, Daewoo was nearly destroyed and the founder Kim Woo Chung forced to resign in 1999.

Korea has seen turbulent times. The relationships with China have not always been peaceful and thus the company's decision to invest in the huge potential of China was economically sensible but still brave. It is that form of bravery and a willingness to take on the established players in the global market that makes Hyundai worthy of study. Its automobiles can be seen on roads across the globe as the company makes progress to joining the global top ten.

India gradually moved from a two-wheel (motorcycle) economy to a four-wheel automobile economy during the late 1980s and the 1990s. It was a sensible move, therefore, of Hyundai to set up an Indian automobile manufacturing facility in 1996. Offering Indian customers a home-built product has proved successful. Hyundai is not alone in operating in India in this way, but its vehicles have proved more popular than some of the older lines whose production facilities have been transferred to Indian factories.

Hyundai has also acquired 51% of the Korean automobile manufacturer Kia. Kia makes vehicles that are fairly basic and at the bottom of the price range. In the early twenty-first century Kia began to expand from the US into Europe. The vehicles have not been well received by the press to date. European motorists are fairly sophisticated and the standard of finish needs to be improved before the brand gains any respectability. Even Chrysler, entering the European family automobile market after their merger with Daimler, had to make considerable improvements to the ride quality and finish of its Neon product before it was acceptable to European buyers – something they have done and are slowly gaining market share. Hyundai vehicles were considered a low-cost purchase in Europe for a long time but have gained in respectability as the products have been improved to take note of customer requirements.

Figure 7.3 shows the timeline for Hyundai.

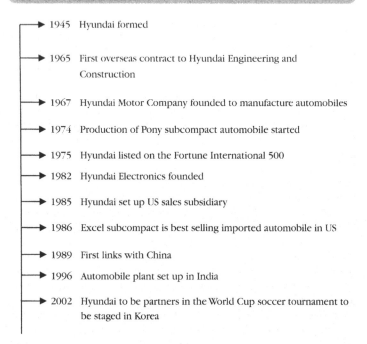

1945 Hyundai formed

1965 First overseas contract to Hyundai Engineering and Construction

1967 Hyundai Motor Company founded to manufacture automobiles

1974 Production of Pony subcompact automobile started

1975 Hyundai listed on the Fortune International 500

1982 Hyundai Electronics founded

1985 Hyundai set up US sales subsidiary

1986 Excel subcompact is best selling imported automobile in US

1989 First links with China

1996 Automobile plant set up in India

2002 Hyundai to be partners in the World Cup soccer tournament to be staged in Korea

Fig. 7.3 Timeline of growth of Hyundai.

HYUNDAI: KEY INSIGHTS

» By listening to the customer and providing what the customer wants, Hyundai was able to grow in twenty years from nothing to producing the highest selling imported automobile into the US.

» Diversification allowed Hyundai to weather the downturn in the Asian economy.

» Moving into China at an early stage gave Hyundai access to potentially the world's biggest market.

Key Concepts and Thinkers on Growth

This chapter provides the following information.

» A glossary of growth and growth-related concepts.
» Details of key thinkers on growth.

A GLOSSARY FOR GROWTH

Acquisitions – The process of growing by gaining an ownership interest in another company. Acquisition can be for the purpose of removing a competitor or diversifying either into a different region or area or a new field of operation. One of the major advantages of growing by acquisition is that the acquired company may well have a loyal customer base that – with careful retention of brands, etc. – can be retained. A disadvantage is that employees who may be used to a different organizational culture will need to be absorbed. Companies are often vulnerable to acquisition at the adolescence, rejuvenation, or decline stages of the organizational life cycle (see below), as they often need injections of cash at these times.

Alliances – Agreements between companies to co-operate in certain areas for mutual benefit. The advantage to a growing company is that it can gain experience in a market without having to set up a full-scale operation. It will, however, be required to share some of its proprietary knowledge with its partners, who may later become competitors. The issue of balance is a delicate one and the whole situation needs careful analysis before such alliances are undertaken.

Business plans – The plan, often financial, which details how the company intends to grow in the short to medium term. Business planning is an important area of managerial activity as the business plan will be the basis for approaches to banks and investors for cash to fund growth. See the *ExpressExec* title *Business Planning* for more details.

Cashflow – The process that charts how cash enters and leaves the company. Most projects require cash to be used for resources before there is any revenue. Mature companies have revenues from established projects that can be used to support new ventures. Whilst orders, etc. can be counted as assets and therefore count towards profit, actual cash is needed to pay bills. Employees and utilities, etc. still need to be paid even though the revenue has not come on-stream. Managing the cashflow to ensure that there is sufficient cash available to meet contingencies is an important part of business planning.

Critical mass – The minimum size of an organization that enables it to operate successfully. It is not possible to give an absolute size for the critical mass required for a particular organization as it depends on the sector within which the organization operates, the size of the market, the relative strength of the competition, etc. Experienced managers, however, can usually recognize when critical mass has been achieved and the organization appears to be able to compete in its own right. Just as there is a lower figure for critical mass there can also be a situation where the organization grows too large to hold together. The larger an organization becomes the harder it becomes to manage. There are so many people in a large organization that the crucial personal contacts become more difficult to establish and then maintain. It may well be that the organization has to divide up into sectors or operating divisions, each part of the whole but run in an independent or semi-independent manner. The method of operation of the Dixons Group members mirrors this situation. To the outside world they may well appear completely separate.

It is often the case that, as a company expands into a wider market, the critical mass required also increases. Joint ventures are a useful method of achieving a temporary increase in the critical mass to enable the company to compete. As joint ventures are often a temporary expedient, the company is able to develop its own necessary critical mass for the particular market.

Culture – The values, attitudes, and beliefs ascribed to and accepted by a group, nation or organization. In effect, "the way we do things around here."

Diversification – A growth mechanism that involves expanding the portfolio of products or services offered, either organically or by acquiring other companies. Horizontal diversification involves expanding into linked products and services, e.g. from TVs to video recorders to hi-fi systems, etc. Vertical diversification is the acquisition of other parts of the value chain. Many vacation companies grow by moving from offering holidays to acquiring airline interests, thus enabling them to offer an airport thru' resort service to their customers.

Grudge purchases – Those purchases such as insurance, law enforcement, funerals, etc. that customers know that they need but resent paying for. Marketing of such services requires an emphasis on the benefits rather than the actual product/service.

ISP (Internet Service Provider) – These companies provide the link between Internet users and the World Wide Web, usually by subscription to their services. AOL (America On Line) is a well-known example.

Internet-specific companies – These are companies set specifically to exploit the capabilities of the Internet. They fall into two categories. Firstly there are those companies that are using the Internet as their prime method of trading (e-commerce), of which Amazon.com is one of the best-known examples. The second category are companies that provide Internet service: this includes the ISPs and search engine providers (see later), and companies such as CISCO. Christopher Price (see Key thinkers) has profiled many of those who have grown companies in this area, and a number of the *Business the . . . Way* books from Capstone (listed in Chapter 9) cover the growth of companies related to Internet activities.

Joint ventures – Temporary alliances (see Alliances) where two or more companies agree to work on specific projects in partnership. Often used when companies from different countries wish to work together.

Organizational life cycle – Similar to the human or product life cycles, the organizational life cycle represents the stages an organization passes through. Those stages are birth, adolescence, maturity, menopause, and either rejuvenation or decline. Growth is most likely to occur at the birth, adolescence, or rejuvenation stages. Organizations in adolescence or decline are vulnerable to acquisition by other organizations seeking to grow as it is at these times that an organization may be in urgent need of cash.

Mergers – Technically different from an acquisition where one company purchases another, in a merger two or more companies come together to form a new entity.

Organic growth – Growth within the organization, usually either by growing larger with the same product/service provision or by diversification (see Diversification.)

Search engines – The method and software used by Internet users to search for pages on the World Wide Web. Webpages are registered with the search engine databases. Yahoo!, Lycos, Excite, etc. provide commonly employed search engines. They are nearly always funded by advertising and are thus free to the user.

Span of control – The number of people an individual can supervise directly. The number is generally reckoned to be between seven and ten, although new technologies may be raising the limit. Above the span of control another hierarchical layer may be necessary.

Transformation process – The process of transforming the inputs to an organization into the outputs that are provided to the customer. The transformation process represents the adding of value that pays for the inputs, overheads, wages, staffing, marketing, etc. and, in the case of companies, provides for a margin of profit, some of which goes to the owners, with the remainder being available for investment.

KEY THINKERS

All of the books referred to in this section are listed fully in Chapter 9.

Anslinger, Patricia L

A co-worker with Thomas Copeland (see Copeland, Thomas), Anslinger is a principal of the McKinsey & Company New York Office. As one of the world's premier consulting firms, McKinsey was responsible for commissioning the research that led to Tom Peters and Bob Waterman writing *In Search of Excellence* – still one of the bestselling business books of all time. Anslinger, together with Copeland, writing in the Harvard Business Review text *Strategies for Growth*, has challenged the perceived wisdom that acquisitions should be based on synergy. They have provided evidence that with care, even non-synergical acquisitions can make a large and swift contribution to a company's bottom line.

Anslinger has contributed to the *Harvard Business Review*, *McKinsey Quarterly* and *Director and Boards*.

Highlights
Books:

» "Growth through Acquisitions", in *Strategies for Growth* (1994) (with Thomas Copeland), Harvard Business Review.

Baghai, Mehrdad

Together with Stephen Coley and David White, Mehrdad Baghai wrote *The Alchemy of Growth* while at McKinsey & Company (see also Anslinger, Patricia L and Copeland, Thomas).

While the word "alchemy" might suggest that growth is a mystical quality, the study of 30 companies provides a practical guide combined with an in-depth understanding of the growth process. The all-important processes of laying foundations and proactively seeking out opportunities show that there is nothing magical about growth - it stems from hard work.

The authors make the point that growth cannot always be continued. One of the complaints that has been made about the ideas of Tom Peters and Bob Waterman (also from McKinsey & Company) in *In Search of Excellence* has been that companies that were doing well in the late 1970s and early 1980s had faltered later on. Baghai *et al.* recognize that since writing *The Alchemy of Growth* in 1999, some of the companies studied have not been as successful in growing as they had been. That does not detract from the lessons that can be learnt. Growth is a function of the present with an anticipation of the future. Sometimes the future can be predicted but in many cases it cannot be - except by hindsight. Growth can slow for reasons totally unconnected with the company. A well-managed company will, however, have the reserves to weather a slump and be ready to grow again when the circumstances are right.

Highlights

Books:

» *The Alchemy of Growth* (1999) (with Stephen Coley and David White)

Coley, Stephen

See Baghai, Mehrdad.

Copeland, Thomas

A co-worker of Patricia Anslinger, Copeland was a professor of finance at UCLA before becoming director of financial services at the consulting firm of McKinsey & ompany in New York. Of particular interest in the context of this material is his work with Anslinger on the benefits of non-synergical growth and the links between finance and policy, described in his 1988 text *Financial Theory and Corporate Policy*.

Highlights

Books:

» *Financial Theory and Corporate Policy* (1988)
» "Growth through Acquisitions", in *Strategies for Growth* (1994) (with Patricia Anslinger), Harvard Business Review.

Lorange, Peter

Peter Lorange, president of IMD in Switzerland and formerly president of the Norwegian School of Management and a teacher at Wharton and MIT, has contributed to the issue of growth through his work with Johan Roos on strategic alliances.

Together they produced the classic text on alliance and joint ventures – *Strategic Alliances* (1992).

The number of such alliances grew rapidly throughout the last decade of the twentieth century, growth that seems set to continue into the twenty-first.

By studying a large number of such operations, Lorange and Roos have been able to generate a blueprint for managing growth through this means. The point is made that the process is one that occurs over time and comprises steps that are commercial, analytical, and political. Lorange and Roos stress the importance of trust in the relationships – not always the easiest task in a competitive environment.

Highlights

Books:

» *Strategic Alliances – Formation, Implementation & Evolution* (1992) (with Johan Roos)
» *The Strategic Planning Process* (1994)

Price, Christopher

Until March 2000, Price was the information technology correspondent of the London *Financial Times*, having worked for the newspaper for 10 years. His first book, *Internet Entrepreneurs*, was published in 2000 and profiles a number of well-known (e.g. Jeff Bezos of Amazon.com) and lesser-known names who have shown their entrepreneurial skills in Internet-related activities. Much of the growth of these companies has been quite spectacular. As they have grown they have had to develop more traditional management structures and there are good examples from Price of how experienced managers have been recruited to support the creative founders of these companies.

Highlights

Books:

» *The Internet Entrepreneurs* (2000)

Roos, Johan

Co-author of *Strategic Alliances* with Peter Lorange, Johan Roos, assistant professor at the Norwegian School of Management, has written extensively on the subject of organizational knowledge and intellectual capital. Given that it is often expertise that is as much sought after in acquisitions as are assets, this is a growing area of research.

Highlights

Books:

» *Strategic Alliances* (1992) (with Peter Lorange)
» *Managing Knowledge* (1996) (co-ed with G von Krogh)
» *Intellectual Common Sense* (1997)
» *Intellectual Capital* (1997)

Tichy, Noel M

Noel M. Tichy is a professor of Organizational Behavior and Human Resource Management at the University of Michigan Business School, where he is the director of the Global Leadership Program and an authority on business growth.

Between 1985 and 1987, Tichy was responsible for management education at General Electric, where he directed its world-wide management development programs. Prior to joining the Michigan Faculty he served for nine years on the Columbia University Business School Faculty. Tichy is the author of numerous books and articles. Of particular interest in the context of this material is his 1998 book *Every Business Is A Growth Business*, written in partnership with Ram Charan. In 1997 he co-authored *The Leadership Engine: How Winning Companies Build Leaders at Every Level* with Eli Cohen, named one of the top ten business books of the year by *Business Week*. He is also the co-author with Stratford Sherman of *Control Your Destiny or Someone Else Will: How Jack Welch is Making General Electric the World's Most Competitive Company* and the author of both *Corporate Global Citizenship* and *Strategic Change Management*, in addition to a number of texts on leadership and human resource management.

Tichy has served on the editorial boards of the *Academy of Management Review*, *Organizational Dynamics*, *Journal of Business Research*, and *Journal of Business Strategy*. He is past chairman of the Academy of Management's Organization and Management Theory Division and is a member of the Board of Governors of the American Society for Training and Development. He was the 1987 recipient of the New Perspectives on Executive Leadership Award by Johnson Smith & Knisely for the most outstanding contribution to the field as captured in *The Transformational Leader*, written with Mary Anne Devanna. He received the 1993 Best Practice Award from the American Society for Training and Development and the 1994 Sales and Marketing Executives International Educator of the Year Award. Tichy is the founder and editor in chief of the *Human Resource Management Journal*. Noel Tichy has been widely consulted by a variety of organizations. He is a senior partner in Action Learning Associates. His clients have included: Ameritech, AT&T, Mercedes-Benz, BellSouth, CIBA-GEIGY, Chase Manhattan Bank, Citibank, Exxon, General Electric, General Motors, Honeywell, Hitachi, Imperial Chemical Inc., IBM, NEC, Northern Telecom, Nomura Securities and 3M.

Highlights

Books:

» *Managing Strategic Change* (1983)

» *Control Your Destiny or Someone Else Will: How Jack Welch is Making General Electric the World's Most Competitive Company* (1994)
» *Every Business Is A Growth Business* (1997)
» *The Leadership Engine: How Winning Companies Build Leaders at Every Level* (1997)
» *Corporate Global Citizenship* (1997)

Walcoff, Philip

Author of *The Fast Forward MBA in Business Planning for Growth*, Walcoff has provided an easy-to-read guide for those seeking to grow their business. Although written for a popular market, Walcoff manages to blend the necessary theoretical vigor into practical steps for planning and growth management. He shows that planning for growth is a process that moves from the identification of issues that are blocking growth into strategies to overcome these barriers to increase both growth and profitability, Finally he stresses the importance of developing a plan. Although the book is under a *Fast Forward MBA* banner it is of as much use to company executives as it is to students.

As president of PWI Business Solutions based in Maryland, Walcoff spends much of his time working with companies of all sizes on the design and implementation of growth strategies.

Highlights

Books:

» *The Fast Forward MBA in Business Planning for Growth* (1999)

White, David

See Baghai, Mehrdad.

Zook, Chris

As a director of Bain & Co., a global consultancy firm, Chris Zook and his colleague James Allen undertook a ten-year study of 2000 companies. They concluded that most growth and most profit came from core activities where the company could exploit its traditional expertise. In many ways this presents a counterpoint to the non-synergical arguments of Anslinger and Copeland (above).

Zook does recognize the importance of what are termed "adjacent opportunities" for diversification, something that both Dixons Group and Wal-Mart (Chapter 7) have proved adept at exploiting.

Profit from the Core is a useful starting point for anybody seeking information about the growth process.

Highlights

Books:

» *Profit from the Core* (2001) (with James Allen)

Resources for Growth

This chapter lists the following information.

» Resources for studying growth.
» General texts.
» Specific texts.
» Journals and magazines.
» Websites.

BOOKS

Note: Dates of books in this chapter may differ from those shown in previous chapters. The dates here are of editions that have been revised from the date of first publication as shown in the chapter material.

Anslinger, P.L. & Copeland, T.E. (1994) "Growth through acquisitions," in *Strategies for Growth*, Harvard Business School, Cambridge (MA).

Baghai, M., Coley, S., & White, D. (1999) *The Alchemy of Growth*, Texere, London.

Bower, T. (2000) *Branson*, 4th Estate, London.

Cartwright, R. (2001) *Communications*, Capstone, Oxford.

Cartwright, R. (2001) *Managing Diversity*, Capstone, Oxford.

Cartwright, R. & Green, G. (1997) *In Charge of Customer Satisfaction*, Blackwell, Oxford.

Collier, P. & Horowitz, D. (1976) *The Rockefellers – an American Dynasty*, Simon & Schuster, New York.

Copeland, T. (1988) *Financial Theory and Corporate Policy*, Addison Wesley, New York.

Lewis, R.D. (2000) *When Cultures Collide*, Nicholas Brealey, London.

Lorange, P. (1994) *The Strategic Planning Process*, Dartmouth, London.

Lorange, P. & Roos, J. (1992) *Strategic Alliances*, Blackwell USA, Cambridge (MA).

Moran, R.T. & Harris, P.R. (2000) *Managing Cultural Differences*, Gulf Publishing Co, Houston.

Peters, T. & Waterman, R. (1982) *In Search of Excellence*, Harper & Row, New York.

Roos, J. (1997) *Intellectual Capital*, Palgrave/Macmillan, Basingstoke (UK).

Roos, J. (1997) *Intellectual Common Sense*, Palgrave/Macmillan, Basingstoke (UK).

Roos, J. & von Krogh, G. (1996) *Managing Knowledge*, Sage, London.

Tichy, N. (1997) *Corporate Global Citizenship*, Jossey Bass, San Francisco.

Tichy, N. (1997) *The Leadership Engine*, HarperCollins, New York.

Tichy, N. (1983) *Managing Strategic Change*, Wiley, New York.

Tichy, N. & Charan, R. (1998) *Every Business is a Growth Business*, Random House, New York.

Tichy, N. & Sherman, S. (1994) *Control your Destiny or Somebody Else Will*, Harper Business, New York.

Trompenaars, F. (1993) *Riding the Waves of Culture*, Economist Books, London.

Waine, P. & Walker, M. (2000) *Takeover*, Wiley, Chichester (UK).

Walcoff, P. (1999) *The Fast Forward MBA in Business Planning for Growth*, Wiley, New York.

Zook, C. & Allen, J. (2001) *Profit from the Core*, Harvard Business School, Cambridge (MA).

For information about Hyundai

Hiscock, G. (2000) *Asia's New Wealth Club*, Nicolas Brealey, London.

For information on the Internet, AOL, and Internet-related growth

Aldrich, D.F. (1999) *Mastering the Digital Marketplace*, Wiley, New York.

Byrd, L. (2001) *Business the Oracle Way*, Capstone, Oxford.

Crainer, S. (2001) *Business the Jack Welch Way*, Capstone, Oxford.

Crainer, S. (2001) *Business the Rupert Murdoch Way*, Capstone, Oxford.

Dearlove, D. (2001) *Business the Bill Gates Way*, Capstone, Oxford.

Dearlove, D. (2001) *Business the Richard Branson Way*, Capstone, Oxford.

Fortier, J. (2001) *Business the Sun Way*, Capstone, Oxford.

Merriden, T. (2001) *Business the Nokia Way*, Capstone, Oxford.

Price, C. (2000) *The Internet Entrepreneurs*, Pearson, London.

Saunders, R. (2000) *Business the Dell Way*, Capstone, Oxford.

Saunders, R. (2001) *Business the Amazon Way*, Capstone, Oxford.

Smith, R. & Vlamis, A. (2000) *Business the Yahoo! Way*, Capstone, Oxford.

Stauffer, D. (2000) *Business the Cisco Way*, Capstone, Oxford.

Stauffer, D. (2000) *Business the AOL Way*, Capstone, Oxford.

For information about Starbucks

Schultz, H. & Yang, D.J. (1997) *Pour Your Heart into it - How Starbucks Built a Company One Cup at a Time*, Hyperion, New York.

For information about Wal-Mart

Quinn, W. (2000) *How Wal-Mart is Destroying America (and the World)*, 10 Speed, Berkeley (CA).

Vance, S.S. & Scott, R.V. (1994) *Wal-Mart - a History of Sam Walton's Retail Phenomenon*, Twayne, New York.

MAGAZINES AND JOURNALS

Those interested in growth should consult the quality newspapers of the areas or countries in which they are interested for details of trends and current affairs pertaining to their areas of operation. Major Western broadsheet-type newspapers - e.g. *The Washington Post, New York Times, Herald Tribune, Times* (London), *Daily Telegraph, Observer, Le Monde*, etc. - provide useful analysis of news and financial/business matters and cover international as well as national news. Current affairs and other relevant programs on the radio or television are useful but, as with newspapers, a translator may be required. Most major newspapers now have an online edition.

The following, most of which are published online as well as in print (see Websites at the end of this chapter), are useful sources of information about markets, competitors, and developments. The Websites should be accessed for subscription rates, samples, and special subscription offers.

Business 2.0

This business and financial daily carries articles etc. of an international nature. The importance of scanning such material for items of possible interest cannot be overstated.

Economist

This is a weekly current affairs magazine with a global approach and thus very useful when considering both growth and the actions of competitors. The *Economist* carries general current affairs news in addition to analysis and market news on a global basis. Issued both as a print version and online. Available by subscription or from newsstands.

Forbes publications

This leading company provides resources for the world's business and investment leaders, providing them with commentary, analysis, relevant tools, and real-time reporting; includes real-time original reporting on business, technology, investing, and lifestyle. *Forbes* magazine is extremely useful reading for all those involved in business as it provides good general intelligence on market trends. The weekly *Forbes* magazine is also available online and, while mainly designed for a US audience, is read on a global basis. It often carries articles and commentaries on growth issues.

Other linked products from Forbes include:

» *Forbes Global* – covering the rise of capitalism around the world for international business leaders. Contains sections on companies and industry; capital markets and investing; entrepreneurs; technology; and *Forbes* global life.
» *Forbes Newsletters* – including the following:
   Forbes Aggressive Growth Investor, a monthly newsletter recommending the 50 best growth and momentum stocks to own now as determined by a proprietary multi-dimensional computer analysis of over 3000 stocks;
   Gilder Technology Report, covering the smartest, most profitable way to invest in technology;
   Special Situation Survey, with monthly stock recommendations, hold or sell advice on each recommendation, and special investment reports (this tends to be of interest mainly to investors in the US stock market, of which there are many in Europe and Asia); and
   New Economy Watch, a newsletter that looks at Internet-based companies.

Harvard Business Review

This leading business and management resource is read world-wide and features contributions by the leading names in business and management. Published 10 times per year and available by subscription. Many of the world's leading authorities on growth have been published in the *Harvard Business Review* and it should be one of the journals that is available to managers throughout the world, so influential are those contributing to it.

Management Today

Issued by the Institute of Management in the UK, monthly to members or by subscription. Often contains useful articles on issues concerned with organizational growth and descriptions of how senior managers have taken their businesses forward.

McKinsey Quarterly

This material has featured a number of members of McKinsey & Company. Each quarter the company publishes an authoritative online journal that contains features and articles, many of which are associated with business growth.

Sloan Management Review

The management journal of MIT (Massachusetts Institute of Technology), this journal attracts some of the world's leading authorities on business and management. Growth and associated issues are a frequent subject of the articles. The range of the journal is global and not confined to the US. The *Sloan Management Review* is published quarterly.

Time

This magazine, while originally a US product, has a global readership and is one of the most important current affairs and commentary magazines in existence. To appear on the cover of *Time* is to have made it; to be the *Time* man or woman of the year is a considerable honor indeed. Time covers a huge range of issues and is thus a useful tool for those involved in business. Whilst not directly targeted at the growing business, a good working knowledge of world events is often a prerequisite to successful growth. The print version is available either on subscription or from newsstands.

ONmagazine.com is the online complement to *ON*, the million-plus monthly personal-tech magazine from the editors of *Time*. The site is a before-you-buy authority on new gadgets and Web services. As such there may be much of interest to a growing business. ONmagazine.com features a new hands-on review every weekday, along with jargon-free how-to-buy guides for popular product categories.

Wall St Journal

This US financial daily carries analysis, financial, and other commercial news, plus company results. Available on subscription or from newsstands. While not directly related to growth, its business and financial coverage is often a good source of information on the growth potential or policies of other listed companies.

TRADE AND PROFESSIONAL JOURNALS

Each company operates in its own sectors and particular marketplace with a set of product, services, or ideas unique to the sector to, at least some extent.

In addition to understanding the general world of business and commerce there will be specific sectoral requirements and knowledge that a company needs to consider when contemplating growth. This is especially important when looking at companies in other sectors that may be being considered for an acquisition.

WEBSITES

www.amazon.com – Amazon.com Website
www.aol.com – America On Line Website
www.business2.com – *Business 2* Website
www.dixons-group-plc.co.uk – Dixons Website.
www.economist.com – *Economist* Website
www.forbes.com – Forbes Website
www.hbsp.harvard.edu/products/hbr – *Harvard Business Review* Website
www.hyundai.com – Hyundai Website
www.inst-mgt.org.uk – Institute of Management Website
www.mckinseyquarterly.com – *McKinsey Quarterly* Website
http://mitsloan.mit.edu – *Sloan Management Review* Website
www.starbucks.com – Starbucks Website
www.time.com – *Time* magazine Website
www.walmartstores.com – Wal-Mart Website

Ten Steps to Managing Growth

The 10 steps to managing growth are:

1 know what you want to do;
2 find out about your customers;
3 find out about your competitors;
4 keep an eye on the cashflow;
5 know when to diversify;
6 know when to acquire;
7 take your people with you;
8 know your investors;
9 stay friends with the bank; and
10 know when to divest.

The 10 steps listed below are those that an organization needs to take if it is to grow successfully and manage that growth effectively. It can be seen from the first few steps that growth needs to be carefully planned – you need to know where you are going, who is going with you, and how far to take it before you start to grow any organization.

1. KNOW WHAT YOU WANT TO DO

Those directing the affairs of any organization, whether in the private or public sector, need to have a clear picture of where they want the organization to go. Growth starts with a vision and a mission that is then implemented through the activities of the organization. Unfocused growth is nearly always transitory. Focus provides the drive to ensure that growth is in line with the vision.

The direction that the organization is taking is not something that should be vested purely in senior management but needs to be communicated to all the stakeholders in the organization so that their efforts can also be focused. The more people who understand the intended direction (including suppliers, customers, bankers, and investors) the more likely it is that the intended results can be achieved.

2. FIND OUT ABOUT YOUR CUSTOMERS

Growth occurs either because there are more customers as a group, or because the existing customer base is using more of the organization's products/services – or a combination of both. Organizations that are customer-centered will find growth easier because the direction in which they choose to grow will be in tune with the needs and wants of the customer base.

Organizations that do not take the trouble to find out about their customers may find that, however technically advanced their products are, they will fail if nobody actually wants them. While this might seem like common sense it was not many years ago that the UK inventor Sir Clive Sinclair launched an ultra-small electric vehicle, the C5, onto the market. Whilst it was a wonderful idea, even the most rudimentary market research might have suggested that a vehicle where the single occupant was in an almost prone position was not best suited to the streets of London, crowded as they are with trucks, cars, taxis, and large double-decker buses. The C5 was a flop – a costly flop. There are still organizations that believe that they can grow the way they want and that the customers will "buy what they are told." This approach is doomed to failure in a free market economy where the customer has a choice.

3. FIND OUT ABOUT YOUR COMPETITORS

A major hotel in Scotland once told delegates at a business seminar that it sent members of staff to stay in other hotels to "CASE" them – Copy And Steal Everything. They did not, of course, mean ashtrays and bath towels. What they wanted the staff to do was to report on new initiatives and levels of service so that the hotel could ensure that it always met the products and standards of its competitors. Sam Walton (see Chapter 7) was renowned for studying the activities of his competitors. There is nothing wrong or unethical about this: airlines, retail operators, car hire companies, etc. all send people out to sample competitor products.

Any organization wishing to grow needs to know what others in the field are doing and to be ready to match them move for move if necessary.

Automobile trading in the UK moved to a much more customer-centered approach during the late 1980s and 1990s. Within just a few years items that had been expensive extras, such as power steering and air-conditioning, instead became standard. Dealers suddenly started offering loan cars and enhanced service overnight. Manufacturers introduced new return policies and extended warranties. It just took one manufacturer to offer extras and the rest were forced to follow whether they wanted to or not. In 2000, Chrysler (following its merger with Daimler) introduced its Neon range to the UK. Automatic transmission is a no-cost extra on the Neon whereas it is an expensive option on other UK vehicles. How long will it be before a competitor also offers it at no cost?

4. KEEP AN EYE ON THE CASHFLOW

The importance of not running out of cash has already been emphasized in this material. It is all too easy to become blinded by the possibility of growth and to forget that it has to be paid for. The revenue stream may take some time to come online and developments, research, marketing, etc. will have to be paid for. Money that has to be borrowed will need to be repaid with interest.

Cash-rich predators may see an opportunity if the company appears to have cashflow problems. Make sure that suppliers know that they will be paid. It only takes one to become worried and demand their money for a run on the company to start.

Running out of cash can be one of the most tragic things that can happen to a company as it can threaten its very survival as an independent entity despite the strength of the order book.

5. KNOW WHEN TO DIVERSIFY

Single product or service companies are extremely vulnerable in the same way that an economy that depends only on a single crop or raw material is. Such a company has no flexibility to cope with changes in market trends.

Companies should consider diversification as their first method of growing. Simple movements into related products and services can often be accomplished with the minimum of risk and a small investment.

Diversification allows the company to remain close to its core activities whilst still being able to grow. Diversification also enables the company to offer extra products/services to its existing customer base whilst also perhaps attracting new customers.

6. KNOW WHEN TO ACQUIRE

Acquisition is a more problematic growth method than diversification. Once a company starts acquiring others it is probable that it will be moving into new markets and areas of operation. In doing so it will need to acquaint itself with the culture and rules of the new market.

The company may also have to integrate employees used to a different regime into its way of doing things – never an easy task. When acquisitions are being made it is important to ensure that new and existing staff are made aware of the strategies that the company is using to accomplish its growth.

7. TAKE YOUR PEOPLE WITH YOU

Ultimately all growth depends on people, particularly customers (see step 2) and employees. In the excitement and dynamism of growth it can be all too easy to forget that there will be those within the company who may not understand what is happening.

Communicating what is happening to employees is a vital and integral part of the growth process. Failure to let employees know what is happening and how the growth process will affect them can be a considerable barrier to growth. People whose energies are being directed at protecting their jobs will have less energy to dedicate to making the growth process as effective as possible

8. KNOW YOUR INVESTORS

Whilst institutional investors may be more interested in immediate returns, many investors wish to have a continuing relationship with the company. Growth may well require asking them for additional funds. It is important, therefore, to keep them fully informed about the decisions being made and the direction the company wishes to take. Although fictional, the novel *Takeover* (details in Chapter 9) by P. Waine and M. Walker is based on real events and shows how growth can be threatened when investors and boards are not appraised fully about what is happening.

9. STAY FRIENDS WITH THE BANK

Step 4 stressed the importance of cashflow. Amongst the best friends a company can have are its bankers. A bank is far more than a place to deposit cash or to ask for a loan. Banks employ analysts who can provide a valuable service to companies, especially those too small to employ their own analysts. If an acquisition is contemplated, bankers can provide a wealth of information and expertise. The bank may even loan a member of staff to work with a company to assist the growth process.

Whenever growth is being planned, the banks should be amongst the first to be consulted. If the growth involves expansion into a new region or country, the network of connections that banks have built up over time will be invaluable. Only the very largest companies can rival the information network that operates within the global banking world and few possess the relationships with governments that banks have.

If problems occur, companies that have kept the banks informed about their plans and their implementation are likely to find that they are treated with much more sympathy and understanding than those companies that have kept the bank at arms length.

Choosing a bank is as crucial as any business process. The relationship between a company and its bankers is likely to be a long and close one. It is worth remembering that it is almost impossible to hide anything about the state of the company's financial health from the banks – they see it all.

10. KNOW WHEN TO DIVEST

This material has been concerned with the management of the growth process. However divestment is an important part of that process. Sometimes, as those reptiles that shed their skin know, divestment of the old is necessary before new growth can occur. All gardeners know the importance of pruning: there are plants that have to be cut back severely to encourage new growth.

Companies – or rather their owners – can become very attached to activities that should be divested. The original activities of a company can acquire an almost mystical significance and be held on to for far longer than is commercially desirable.

Part of the planning process should be to examine the company's full portfolio to see if there are products, services, or even constituent companies that should be divested. Sentiment should have no place in this analysis. A resource-draining operation may be capable of sale and this can generate funds to support growth in other areas.

External advisors, such as banks, can be of considerable assistance in this process as they can take a more holistic, less emotional view of what should go and what should stay. It may well be that another company can make a success of a current resource-draining operation.

Growth is a process not of pure addition but one whereby more is added than is removed.

KEY LEARNING POINTS

Organizations that are growing must:

» have a vision;
» analyze the environment;
» keep track of the cash;
» keep stakeholders informed; and
» be prepared to divest themselves of unprofitable activities.

Frequently Asked Questions (FAQs)

Q1: Is growth always to be desired?

A: There are those, often the owners of small businesses, who have no wish for that business to grow. The problem is that they become very vulnerable. Growth provides not only more money but also more influence. The larger an organization is, the more it can demand discounts by purchasing in bulk. In general terms, even if you do not wish your business to expand hugely, some growth is always better than just standing still. If business becomes temporarily depressed there may well be "some meat still on the bone" if the organization has grown. All businesses need a critical mass to survive (see Chapter 8). If they are only just at the critical size, any slowdown in business can put them in danger of not being large enough to survive at all.

The nature of growth is covered in Chapters 1, 2, and 6, while critical mass is to be found in the glossary in Chapter 8.

Q2: How can modern technology, especially the Internet, aid growth?

A: The Internet has speeded up both the process of communication and the ease with which information can be acquired. There is little reason for any organization to claim that they were unable to find out published details about competitors, potential partners, suppliers, etc. – there are few companies of any note that do not possess a Webpage. The Webpages for the companies used as cases in this material can be found at the end of Chapter 9.

The Internet also allows companies to grow by servicing a much larger customer base than was possible before e-commerce.

There is more about the e-dimension to managing growth in Chapter 4.

Q3: What is the link between growth and competition?

A: Paradoxically, competition can aid growth. A major advertising campaign by one supplier very often boosts the market for all the players. Competition also acts as a catalyst for growth. Companies in a highly competitive market that do not grow are actually decreasing in size relative to their competitors and may become extremely vulnerable. See Chapter 2 for the points of vulnerability in the organizational life cycle.

Q4: What different types of growth are there?

A: Growth can occur in a number of ways. It may be that the customer base is expanded by selling the same products or services in new regions or countries. The company may decide to diversify horizontally or vertically, adding either complementary products and services or new parts of the supply chain. It is also possible to acquire other companies whose operations can be added to the core activities. There is more information on this in Chapter 6.

Q5: What dangers are there in growth?

A: The biggest dangers are of running out of cash or stimulating a demand that the company cannot then meet. The former may lead to those who are owed money deciding to call in the debt before the revenue stream comes online; the latter may lead to customers transferring their business to a competitor who can meet their requirements. Lost customers are often lost forever. A simple piece of mathematics shows that if company A loses 10 customers to company B then the relative net gain by organization B over company A is not 10 but 20.

(If both had 100 customers to start with, company A now has 90 and company B has 110, i.e., a difference of +20). See Chapter 6 for further details.

Q6: Can any organization grow?

A: There is no reason why any organization cannot grow. Nevertheless there are those that fail to do so. This may be because the owners are happy with the organization as it is or it is serving a very small, specialized market. The reason for most failures to grow is, however, a lack of appreciation of what is required to initiate and manage the growth process. There can even be considerable growth in grudge purchase areas as the retailers of insurance products can demonstrate. The pre-selling of funeral packages shows that, with careful stressing of the benefits to the deceased's family, even the ultimate grudge product – one's own funeral – can present a growth opportunity for the funeral directing business. Chapters 4, 5, and 7 provide case studies on how a variety of organizations have grown.

Q7: How can growth be measured?

A: For organizations with a profit motive, growth can be measured in financial terms and in the number of employees and customers. Profit, revenue, and return on investment are all financial measures that are employed. A growth in staff employed or in customers is of little use without the likelihood of a rise in profits. Profits may be sacrificed in the short term in order to build up market share. Many Japanese companies used this strategy when penetrating the US and European markets. As prices rise once market share has been achieved, profits should be generated. This approach to growth requires investors who are interested in the long-term prospects of the company.

The growth of organizations in the public sector cannot be measured by profit and may be considered in terms of spending, client numbers, or staff size increases. See Chapter 6 for details.

Q8: Should an organization hang on to all it has?

A: As covered in step 10 of Chapter 10, it is often a good thing to divest oneself of resource-draining operations. An operation that is draining resources is actually producing "negative growth" and holding the real growth of the company back. Divestment is covered in Chapter 6 and it should be noted that Dixons (Chapter 7) has never been loathe to divest itself of a part of the business that no longer fits into the portfolio, even if it has been a long-standing part of the group.

Q9: Is growth infinite?

A: It is not possible for an organization to grow forever and retain its original form. Continued growth over a long period is possible but the structure of the organization is likely to change and the rate of growth will, in all probability, slow down. A period of stability every so often in order to take stock is no bad thing.

Consider this in relation to the organizational life cycle in Chapter 2.

Q10: Where are resources available to assist in understanding the process of managing growth?

A: A list of books, journals and Web addresses is provided in Chapter 9.

Index